Treasures of the
SMITHSONIAN

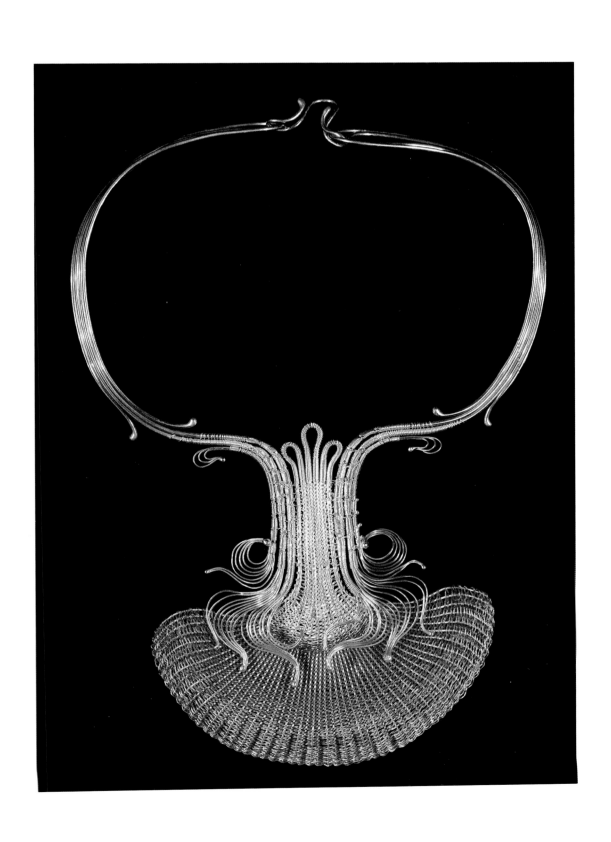

Treasures of the
SMITHSONIAN

General Editor: John S. Bowman

BISON GROUP

First published in 1992 by
Bison Books Ltd
Kimbolton House
117A Fulham Road
London SW3 6RL

ISBN 0-86124-951-8

Printed in Hong Kong

Page 1 Choker # 38, Mary Lee Hu, 1978
(National Museum of American Art)
Page 3 Two Discs, Alexander Calder, 1965
(Hirshhorn Museum and Sculpture Garden)
Page 4 Parvati, Chola dynasty, tenth century AD
(Freer Gallery of Art)

Contents

Introduction

The Smithsonian Institution is an independent establishment devoted to education, research and public service in the arts, sciences and history. For many Americans the word 'Smithsonian' conjures up the image of an archaic-looking castle on the Mall in Washington DC, but in the century and a half since it was founded, the Smithsonian Institution has grown far beyond the bounds of that building. Today it is the largest complex of museums, art galleries and research facilities in the world.

The Smithsonian's collections reflect virtually every area of human interest. Here a visitor can find such diverse delights as a lunar rock that can be touched, President Teddy Roosevelt's original 'Teddy Bear', Muhammad Ali's boxing gloves and a fossilized skeleton of Diplodocus, giant of the dinosaurs. There are masterworks of art from ancient and modern civilizations around the world, dazzling gems of incalculable worth, colorful turn-of-the-century locomotives, automobiles and aircraft. Collectors of stamps, coins, rocks, fine furniture, political campaign paraphernalia, almost anything, will find the ultimate collection at the Smithsonian.

The quality, of course, is stunning, but the quantity is almost beyond comprehension; the museums hold over 137 million objects. New specimens, artifacts, artworks and other items are added at the rate of about half a million a year. While some objects are purchased, many large collections are donated, and every day curators receive calls from generous citizens who have uncovered a treasure or two from the attic that the Smithsonian cannot do without. Sometimes these items pass the test for acceptance, but exhibition is a different matter. The one million items on display at any one time represent only a tiny fraction of the Smithsonian's holdings. While many exhibits are rotated regularly, most of the vast store of scientific, artistic and historic items entrusted to the Institution remain unseen by the public, and are used to further scholarly research.

The 14 museums that make up the Smithsonian repeatedly reach beyond their boundaries and defy their own definitions. Where culture and knowledge meet, a certain blending takes place; art, science, history and nature often overlap. A 'nature' museum displays the artwork of many civilizations, while a 'history' museum shows off crafts, along with technological marvels created through science. An 'art' museum exhibits portraits of historical figures, and in the hi-tech building where airplanes and spacecraft hang from ceilings, a gallery is also devoted to paintings and other art of the aerospace age.

Any visitor who attempts to view all the wonders on display at any one time would find his or her work fascinating, educational, rewarding – and certainly quite daunting. The Smithsonian is many places, and the possibilities it offers seem infinite.

The Smithsonian Institution originated with a half-million dollar bequest in 1829 from an English scientist, James Smithson, who never visited the United States. Smithson was born of royal blood, the illegitimate son of the Duke of Northumberland and Elizabeth Keate Macie, a descendant of King Henry VII. He

Below James Smithson (1765-1829) was the Englishman whose bequest led to establishing the Smithsonian Institution.

Right The dome above the Mall, Washington, DC, marks the Smithsonian's National Museum of Natural History.

inherited his money (then considered a vast sum) mainly from his mother. When he died a childless bachelor at the age of 65, Smithson's will was found to contain an odd stipulation: his fortune was left to his nephew, but if the nephew were to die without heirs, the bequest would then go to the United States of America. Six years later, Smithson's nephew also died, leaving no progeny, and the half-million dollar legacy became the property of the United States. The wording of the will left much open to question, specifying only that the fortune be used 'to found at Washington, under the name of the Smithsonian Institution, an Establishment for the increase and diffusion of knowledge among men.'

Congress did not accept the money easily. Some members felt it was undignified for the United States to take such a substantial gift from a foreigner, and a long debate ensued. This opposition was finally overruled, and in 1838 the funds – in the form of gold sovereigns – were collected by President Andrew Jackson and placed in the Philadelphia Mint.

'Increase and diffusion of knowledge among men' – what did James Smithson mean? Congress argued and reargued the question, fighting over various proposals as to how the money should be spent: a new university,

a national library, an astronomical observatory, a school for training teachers, and a great laboratory were among the suggestions. In 1846, after eight years of disharmonious debate, a bill was passed creating a separate corporate entity, 'the Establishment', to undertake the charge of the Smithson will, as Congress determined that the federal government did not have authority to do so directly. This body in effect constituted the Smithsonian Institution; it consists of the President of the United States, the Vice-President, the Chief Justice and the heads of the executive departments. A Board of Regents was then created to administer the Institution; this included the Vice-President, the Chief Justice and six citizen members among its number. The post of Secretary, effectively chief executive, of the Institution was also established from the outset, the office-holder serving also as Secretary of the Board of Regents.

The plans stipulated a building with 'suitable rooms or halls for the reception and arrangement, upon a liberal scale, of objects of natural history, including a geological and mineralogical cabinet; also a chemical laboratory, a library, a gallery of art, and the necessary lecture rooms . . .' James Renwick, who also designed St Patrick's Cathedral in New York, was named archi-

Left A view of part of the Enid Haupt Garden at the rear of the so-called Castle, the original building of the Smithsonian Institution, designed by James Renwick in the style of a Norman castle. It now houses the Smithsonian's administrative offices and the Woodrow Wilson International Center for Scholars.

Right This lifesize fiberglass model of a Triceratops dinosaur, known as 'Uncle Beazley,' sits in front of the National Museum of Natural History; children are welcome to climb on it.

tect, and the 'suitable' Smithsonian Institution building rose on the Mall in Washington. It was designed as a twelfth-century Norman castle, an asymmetrical red sandstone structure with towers and turrets, battlements, gables and arches. By 1855 it was ready to be occupied. Dr Joseph Henry, a prominent Princeton physicist, somewhat reluctantly accepted the position of first Secretary and moved in with his family, along with a collection of mineral specimens from Smithson's original bequest.

Henry's main goal for the Institution was to further scientific research, and he resisted becoming simply a keeper of objects. 'There is indeed no plan by which the funds of an Institution may be more inefficiently expended,' he wrote, 'that that of filling a costly building with an indiscriminate collection of objects of curiosity . . . ' But by 1857 he was pressured into accepting donations of other collections, and these kept coming. A fire swept through the upper story of the Castle in 1865 and destroyed many important specimens and artworks, but by the time of Joseph Henry's death in 1878, so many collections had been contributed to the Smithsonian by private donors and government agencies that the building was nearly overflowing.

His successor was, in fact, an inveterate naturalist and collector. Spencer Fullerton Baird had gathered a great multitude of ornithological specimens by the age of nineteen, including birds passed on to him by J. J. Audubon himself. Baird eventually switched to ichthyology and amassed a similarly huge collection of fish. When he took over the helm of the Smithsonian in 1878, he brought with him several thousand natural objects. All these items, together with a trainload of modern-day wonders left over from the 1876 Philadelphia Centennial Exhibition, prompted a new museum to be erected in 1881 next to the Castle. Baird organized many collection and research expeditions, and the newly-built National Museum (now the Arts and Industries Building) was soon also filled to capacity.

The Smithsonian was soon to broaden its horizons further. Upon Baird's death in 1887, Samuel Pierpont Langley was appointed Secretary, focusing the Smithsonian on the skies. Langley was a hands-on scientist/ inventor who was fascinated with aeronautics, astronomy and astrophysics. His 1896 Aerodrome, a steam-driven model plane with a 13-foot wingspan, was the first American-powered, heavier-than-air machine that flew a significant distance. With President McKinley's backing, Langley experimented with manned flight but failed, a defeat which troubled him for the rest of his life. He did, however, successfully found the Smithsonian Astrophysical Observatory, beginning a new direction for the Institution.

Paleontologist Charles Doolittle Walcott, the next Secretary, continued Langley's aerospace interests, supporting experiments in rocketry prior to and during World War I. Together with Alexander Graham Bell, he petitioned Congress to open an aeronautical research and policy center, which in 1915 resulted in the National Advisory Committee for Aeronautics, the forerunner of NASA. Walcott also brought in some of the vast collections of fossils now in the National Museum of Natural History. The museum opened in 1911 to house the millions of natural items the Smithsonian by then owned. In 1923 a philanthropic gesture added the Freer Gallery of Art, built to house the collection of oriental and American art donated by Detroit industrialist Charles Lang Freer.

The period between the late 1920s and the early 1950s was a less active time for the Smithsonian, as the nation went through the Depression era, World War II and the period of post-war recovery. But by the end of the 1950s, with the country on the move and growing again, another new museum marked the beginning of a new era for the Smithsonian.

The National Museum of History and Technology (now renamed the National Museum of American History) was finished in 1964. Large, functional and contemporary, it took over many of the dusty exhibits

Left Located outside the National Air and Space Museum is *Delta Solar*, by the contemporary Venezuelean sculptor, Alejandro Otera. The stainless steel structure is filled with rotary sails that create changing reflections in the pool as they move with the wind. The sculpture was presented to the USA on the bicentennial in 1976.

Right above One of the prize displays in the Freer Gallery of Art is the Peacock Room, originally (1876-77) painted for the London home of shipping magnate Frederick Leyland by the American expatriate artist James McNeill Whistler, and later installed in the Washington museum. The most striking image is of the two fighting peacocks; it is said that the one with the upraised tail represents the rich Leyland, the other the impoverished Whistler.

Right below Typical of the early displays in the Museum of Natural History is this beautiful, large butterfly, *Papilio Homerus*, a swallowtail found only in Jamaica. It is here pictured being held by the butterfly expert William Schaus when it was acquired in 1926.

from the Arts and Industries Building and gave them a fresh presentation. Times were changing, and everything in the Smithsonian began to be re-organized or else cleaned off – including the African bush elephant in the Museum of Natural History, whose aged dust was considered 'historic' by curators.

Since 1964, the Smithsonian has experienced enormous broadening and growth. Under S Dillon Ripley's tenure as Secretary, the Institution's interests diversified greatly and many innovative museums were founded. Some were housed in beautifully restored old buildings, two of them saved just in time from demolition. Others were built as modern structures designed to reflect and enhance their collections. The years 1967 through 1976 saw the opening of the Anacostia Neighborhood Museum, a community museum focusing on Afro-American history and culture; the National Museum of American Art; the National Portrait Gallery; the Renwick Gallery, a museum of American crafts, design and decorative arts; the Hirshhorn Museum and Sculpture Garden; the National Air and Space Museum; and the Cooper-Hewitt National Museum of Design in New York City.

In 1987, under the stewardship of Robert McC Adams, the Quadrangle complex was completed, an underground masterpiece of modern architecture which includes the National Museum of African Art and the Arthur M Sackler Gallery. The end of the century will see the re-opening of New York's National Museum of the American Indian in a new museum on the Washington Mall. In addition to these, the branches of the Smithsonian Institution spread out in many directions of knowledge and culture. The Zoological Park in Washington, for example, not only attracts millions of visitors but also serves as a refuge for rare and endangered species of animal. As a research and education complex, the Smithsonian runs observatories, laboratories, environmental study and conservation centers both in the US and overseas. Under its auspices are also the National Gallery of Art, the John F Kennedy Center for the Performing Arts, the Woodrow Wilson International Center for Scholars and the Archives of American Art.

In public service, the Smithsonian labs help police and the FBI to solve crimes; its scientists report on earthquakes, volcanoes and tidal waves; and its curatorial staff will assist any caller with a question about a

piece of art or historical object in his possession. The Institution reaches out to the public with touring exhibits, theatre and dance programs, publications and concerts – as well as with a great carousel, which is wheeled out to the Mall every summer so that children and adults may enjoy a carefree ride.

The original Castle now serves as a visitor information center, and millions of people pass through its portals each year. Inside the door is James Smithson's crypt, which was moved there in 1904. Many stop for a moment to look and wonder. No one will ever know exactly why he left his bequest to a country he had never seen, or what he really had in mind for 'the Smithsonian Institution, an Establishment for the increase and diffusion of knowledge.' But no doubt, he would be satisfied.

This book focuses on eleven Smithsonian museums which are part of the experience of many visitors to Washington, DC and which between them constitute a rich and diverse national treasury.

Above The sound of the whistle of *Old John Bull*, the oldest complete working locomotive in the United States, was broadcast as the locomotive was installed in the Arts and Industries Building in 1931, the 100th anniversary of the train's first run in the USA.

Left A curator examines a Sharp Gothic shelf clock, (c. 1835), one of several rare clocks donated to the Smithsonian Institution in 1931.

Right above This carved walrus tusk is a fine example of scrimshaw – carving on animal ivory. It was made by Eskimo inhabitants of the Bering Sea region and is on display at the Museum of Natural History.

Right below A display in 1931 in the Smithsonian includes the giant dinosaur, a Diplodocus, and the skeleton of a mastodon.

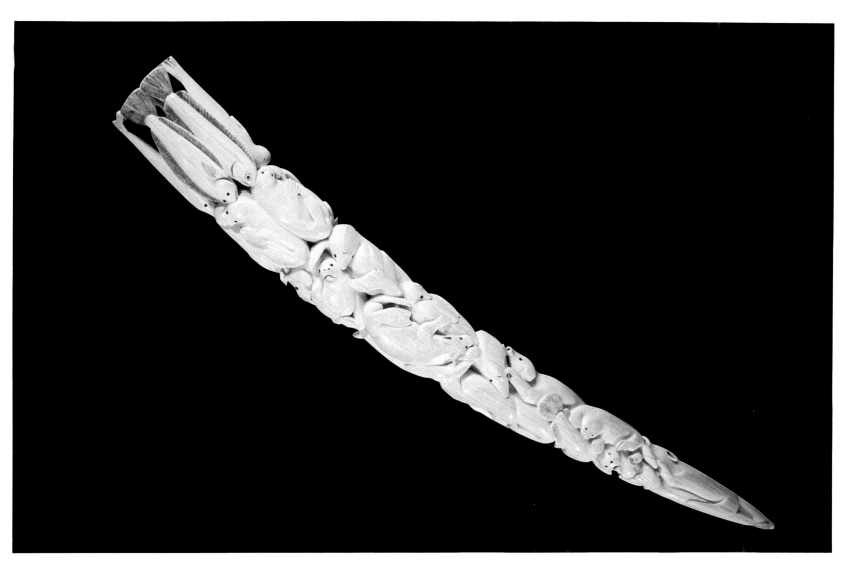

CHAPTER ONE

National Museum of African Art

The predecessor of the National Museum of African Art was founded in 1964 as a private institution in Washington DC by Warren M Robbins, and set up in the old Capitol Hill house of black abolitionist Frederick Douglass. Robbins, a former Foreign Service officer with a love of African cultures, wanted to encourage a deeper appreciation of a continent that still seemed remote to many Americans. His unique Museum of African Art, with its thousands of sculptures, musical instruments, and artifacts, opened in 1964 and became part of the Smithsonian in 1979. Two years later, its name was prefixed by the official word 'National.' In 1987, as part of the new Quadrangle complex, the museum reopened in its ample underground quarters, with sufficient gallery space to display the fine collection. This now includes 6000 objects, as well as the Eliot Eliofsen archives of 300,000 photographic images of African art and culture.

While Westerners may think of Africa as a unified continent, it actually contains about 900 distinct cultures. At the National Museum of African Art, the focus is on artworks and artifacts belonging to cultures south of the Sahara, including the peoples in Zaire, Angola, Ghana, Nigeria, Mali and the Ivory Coast.

African art provides a wonderfully rich contrast to Western art. It is meant to be held, touched and used, not simply admired from a respectable distance. It is three-dimensional: sculpted or woven, carved or modeled. Sculptures have stylized, exaggerated features, while masks are very often frightening – but then, they are meant to be. This is an art of action and life, and it radiates energy and power.

The works often serve a spiritual and religious function; they are also ceremonial, marking such rites of passage as birth, the transition from childhood into adulthood, marriage or death. In African cultures, where spirituality is a part of daily living, a certain blending occurs; art, music, dance, ceremony and religion are nearly inseparable as a fundamental part of life. Objects such as ritual masks, maternity figures, altars to guardian spirits or divination baskets were used by their owners as elements in rituals intended to regulate social life, initiate youths into adulthood, bring on fertility or make sick people well again. Also, and very importantly, they connect the realms of the living with those of the dead, ensuring the afterlife.

As in all cultures, some forms of African art reflect simple functions. Drinking and cooking vessels may be highly decorative, and such items as wooden headrests, used in place of pillows, take shape as beautifully sculpted pieces. Other pieces were created with a social or political purpose, as emblems of rank and leadership. Political leaders used symbolic costumes made of special cloth, and jewelry which included elaborate bracelets, anklets, pendants and rings.

Remarkable examples of art commemorating social status can be seen in the museum's collection of copper-alloy sculptures from the royal kingdom of Benin. Benin, located in the tropical rain forest region now a part of Nigeria, probably dates to the fourteenth century. It was a highly sophisticated society with a system of royal art patronage and wealthy and powerful guild-like groups. Finely crafted sculptures from the sixteenth century onward include depictions of high ranking persons and especially of the *Oba,* the divine ruler who held the power of life and death.

Unfortunately, much remains unknown about African art: centuries-old works have not survived in large numbers. Nature seems to have conspired against art, as most African art objects are made of wood and other organic materials, which do not usually last for more than a hundred years in the continent's tropical climate, and much of the work created over generations and centuries has been lost. For this reason most of the holdings of the Museum of African Art are quite modern, dating from after about 1800; only the relatively few pieces made of stone, terracotta or metal are more than about two hundred years old.

While research into Africa's art history is ongoing, a great deal may never be completely understood. Records were kept only through oral traditions, and early Western explorers failed to take back much information about the prizes they collected. Individual artists remain unnamed and dating is not exact.

For the historian and researcher, this presents an ongoing quest and challenge. Some facts may be gleaned through scientific tests and archeological study, but much must be surmised. Yet surmise is probably not too far off the mark; many of the ancient ceremonies and traditional arts of Africa continue to this day. And through older African sculptures, masks and ritual objects, the spirits still seem to speak.

Above The entrance pavilion to the National Museum of African Art is located behind the Castle, the original building and still the headquarters of the Smithsonian Institution. The vast collection of sub-Saharan art and artifacts is in underground rooms.

Right The core of the holdings of the National Museum of African Art is the collection of Warren M Robbins, an American diplomat who donated it to the Smithsonian in 1979. But decades before that, the Smithsonian itself collected some African art; here, for example, are ceremonial masks from the Ibo tribes of West Africa as they were being acquired by the Smithsonian in 1931.

Left

Figure (Nikishi)
Songye peoples, Zaire
Wood, metal, shell, accumulative
materials, height 26 inches (66 cm)
Museum Purchase and gift of Professor
David Driskell, Friends of the National
Museum of African Art, Robert and
Nancy Nooter, Milton F Frieda
Rosenthal, Hon. and Mrs Michael
Samuels and Mr Michael Sonnenreich
(86.4.1)

This so-called Nikishi figure was
carved by an artist of the Songye
peoples of Zaire; as with most African
art, its exact age is unknown, but its
decorative elements – the shell
jewelry, the gourd, the metal – were
added over time, probably by people
seeking to use the figure to gain some
magic powers. African sculptures
such as this were regarded as functional, not aesthetic; they were used in
various ways, more like fetishes, and
were often passed around from hand
to hand. Like most traditional African
sculptures, this one stands in a rigidly
frontal pose. The head, important as
the origin of the intellect and of the
senses, is often given an exaggerated
size, one-third or more the size of the
full figure.

Above

Headrest
Luba peoples, Zaire
Wood, height 6¾ inches (17 cm)
Museum purchase (86.12.14)

This wooden headrest, made by a
member of the Luba peoples who live
in present-day Zaire, is an example of
how African artist-craftsmen can turn
functional objects into works of sig-
nificance, elegance, and even some
wit. Used as a pillow, it would protect an elaborate hairdo as the person
slept. The two women holding the
rest are bare-chested but their bodies
are adorned and their own hair is care-
fully in place; arms around each
other's waist, they lend support to
each other as they hold the headrest
with their free hands. So although
these women kneel and are clearly ser-
vants of some prestigious individual,
they have their own dignity.

Left
Figure 1908 or earlier
Bamum peoples, Cameroon
Wood, brass, glass beads, cowrie shells
Gift of Evelyn A J Hall and John A
Freede (85.8.1)

This colorful figure was made by a
member of the Bamum, or Baunum,
tribe, who live in Cameroon, in west
central Africa; its maker lived in Fum-
ban, or Foumban, one of the largest
cities in Cameroon. Carved from
wood, the figure was then covered
with red, blue and white beads and
embellished with cowrie shells, once
used as money in sub-Saharan Africa.
Features such as the shape of the cap,
the jewelry and a brass facial sheath
are signs of status, as is its lifessize:
most African sculptures are small
enough to be picked up and handed
around. Unlike so many African
works, this can be dated as no later
than 1908 for it was in that year that
King Njoja of Bamum gave the figure
as a grave marker for a German
colonial officer who had been close to
the king.

Above left
Figure of Woman and Child,
collected before 1914
Yombe group, Kongo peoples
Wood, mirror, glass inlay, glass beads,
metal, height 10⅛ inches (25.7 cm)
Museum purchase with funds provided
by the Smithsonian Institution
collections acquisitions program in 1983
(83.3.6)

This figure of a woman and child was
made by a member of the Yombe
group of the Kongo peoples who in-
habit the region of present-day
Congo and Zaire. Carved from
wood, it was embellished with glass
inlay, a piece of mirror, glass beads,
and metal. It is believed to date from
sometime in the late nineteenth
century. The chief's hat on the
woman's head, unusual when worn
by a female, here symbolizes the importance of maternity and possibly
the status of the child's parents.
Child-bearing ability has been an important measure of success in traditional African societies. Figures of
women and children represent both
maternity and fertility.

Above right
Mask (Pwo)
Muzuamba style, Chokwe
peoples
Wood, fiber, metal, height 15⅜ inches
(39 cm)
Museum purchase (85.12.20)

This mask, made of wood, fiber and
metal, is in the Muzuamba style of the
Chokwe people who live in present-
day Zaire and Angola. Masks, some
with nearly naturalized features such
as this, others wildy exaggerated and
frightening, play an essential part in
traditional African rituals and ceremonies. In West and Central Africa,
masks may be used to call to super-
natural beings as the wearer becomes
possessed by the mask's spirit.
Magical ceremonies are performed by
costumed, masked dancers, often
joined by instrumental musicians and
a chorus of singers. Rites and rituals
that use masks may celebrate an important transition such as the birth of a
child, entrance into adulthood, or
death; other masked ceremonies may
be held to promote human fertility or
a fine harvest.

Left
Equestrian Figure, eighth/
eleventh century
Inland Delta region, Niger River,
Mali
Fired clay, height 27½ inches (70.4 cm)
Museum purchase (86.12.2)

This equestrian figure comes from the
inland delta region in present-day
Mali. It is made of terracotta that has
been lightly painted. Since most
African objects are made from wood
and do not survive the ravages of the
tropical climate over the centuries –
hot, humid weather, destructive insects – this is especially valuable
because of its antiquity: it is dated to
between the 8th-11th centuries AD
(although it has been somewhat re-
constructed). Nigeria is the source of
the most ancient African art objects –
terracotta pieces 2,000 years old. The
elegant equestrian figure may represent a member of the cavalry belonging to a royal court in a highly
advanced urban society that is
described in early Arab documents.

Above
Male head, late fourteenth/early
fifteenth century
Cast copper alloy, iron inlay, height
8¾ inches (22.2 cm)
Purchased with funds provided by the
Smithsonian Institution collections
acquisitions program in 1982 (82.5.2)

This head is from the Royal Kingdom
of Benin that once flourished in the
tropical rain forest area where Nigeria
now exists. The Royal Kingdom of
Benin has a remarkable cultural
history. Lasting from about the
mid-1400s to the mid-1600s, the kingdom was led by the all-powerful *oba*
or king, and was a society that vied for

prestige and riches. Craftsmen and
artists belonged to groups similar to
European guilds, through which they
grew in wealth. Many sophisticated
sculptures were made of brass,
bronze, or other alloys of copper and
were cast under a system of royal
patronage that encouraged skill in the
arts. This superb example of a com-
memorative head dates to the
fifteenth or sixteenth century.
Slightly smaller than life-size, it may
represent a Benin chief or a defeated
king. Unlike so many African sculptures, with their exaggerated features,
the art from the Kingdom of Benin
employs a more subdued, even realistic, if stylized, style.

CHAPTER TWO

National Air and Space Museum

The National Air and Space Museum (NASM) is a place of fantasies, quests and thrilling successes. Attracting 10 million visitors each year, it is the Smithsonian's most popular museum. Streamlined jet planes hang from the ceiling; colorful balloons hover aloft; and giant rockets seem to soar toward the skies. A planetarium simulates the heavens, while stunning films that re-create flight on a five-story-high screen provide thrills for armchair pilots and astronauts.

Since the turn-of-the-century experiments of the Smithsonian's third Secretary, astrophysicist Samuel Pierpoint Langley, the Institution has been intimately involved in aeronautics research and exploration. Langley invented a scaled-down plane that flew 3000 feet with no passenger, but when he attempted a manned flight in 1903, he failed, and the Wright brothers learned from his mistakes. The efforts of Charles Doolittle Walcott, the next Smithsonian Secretary, brought about the National Advisory Committee for Aeronautics (the forerunner of NASA) in 1915. Walcott also encouraged and helped finance the experiments of Robert H Goddard, who is considered the father of modern rocketry. A model of Goddard's earliest small rocket, which went up only 41 feet and yet led to space exploration, is on display at the Air and Space Museum.

In 1946 Congress established the National Air Museum to 'memorialize the national development of aviation.' In 1966, just three years before the United States landed men on the moon, 'Space' also became part of its mandate. The new museum opened in 1976. Built out of pink Tennessee marble and large expanses of glass, it lets in great chunks of the skies.

On December 17, 1903, in a kite-like wood and canvas airplane with a simple motor and bicycle-chain drive, Orville and Wilbur Wright made the first powered, controled, manned flights of a heavier-than-air craft. Orville's maiden 'voyage' lasted all of 12 seconds and 120 feet. It received little immediate attention from the press, but was nonethless a major historical landmark.

Further achievements in flight followed within an incredibly short span of time. Just twenty-five years later, Charles Lindbergh made the first solo flight across the ocean from New York to Paris in a single engine plane. In another twenty years, test pilot

Charles Yeager flew his jet Bell X-1 faster than the speed of sound. And on July 20, 1969, only 66 years after Wright's tentative skip above the sand dunes in *Kitty Hawk Flyer*, Neil Armstrong took his famous step on the surface of the moon.

It is no wonder that visitors to the National Air and Space Museum often feel awestruck upon first passing through its doors. For there they are, the actual crafts that have carried America's aviation and space pioneers, separated from each other by just a few dozen feet: the fragile Wright *Flyer*, Lindbergh's small silver *Spirit of St Louis*, Yeager's orange *Glamorous Glennis* (named for his wife), and the capsule of the Apollo 11 command module *Columbia* that orbited the moon.

Once the way was opened, many daredevils, scientists, explorers and at least a few heroes and heroines felt their allure. Very soon, industries, governments and military establishments sought ways to use them. One of the daredevils was Galbraith Perry Rodgers, a sometime motorcycle racer who completed the first transcontinental flight across the United States in 1911. Rodgers made 69 stops between New York and California and crashed his Wright EX 19 times, arriving at his destination 40 days after he began. His well--restored *Vin Fiz*, a flying advertisement for the soft drink company that sponsored him, is in NASM's collection.

The world's first military plane, the Wright 1909 *Military Flyer* is an antique woodframe bi-plane. During World War I aircraft became far more sophisticated, rapidly evolving from crude observation craft to advanced fighters. The museum has examples of Allied SPADs known for their ability to make fast dives, as well as a German Fokker, a highly respected plane capable of a variety of quick maneuvers. With the advances in technology gained during the war, new records were soon being set, experimental flights were undertaken, and the mails were transported in a new way, by airmail. During the 1920s open-cockpit biplanes such as the Pitcairn *Mailwing* and the Douglas M-2 mailplane were darting around the country and air travel was going commercial.

In 1927, twenty-five-year old mail pilot Charles Lindbergh made the first crossing of the Atlantic. Against the odds, in foul weather, lifting his brow muscles to keep his eyelids open against sleep, Lind-

Above The National Air and Space Museum, located between Jefferson Drive and Independence Avenue, opened in 1976.

bergh flew from New York to Paris. His solo flight in the tiny single-engine Ryan M-2 *Spirit of St Louis* lasted 33 hours and 30 minutes. Thousands were there to greet him; Lindbergh became the great, solitary hero of aviation and inspired countless others to fly.

As a result flight began its 'golden age.' Air races were held, aerobatic flyers made headlines, and technology grew ever more advanced. The Air and Space Museum has many beautiful, brightly-colored craft from the late 1920s and 1930s, including the yellow Beech Model C17L Staggerwing, the red midget *Wittman* Buster, and one of the racers owned by tycoon Howard Hughes.

Meanwhile, during this period, mail-delivery flights were taking on passengers, and planes were soon a new form of transportation for travellers. Suspended from the ceiling of the Hall of Transportation in the museum is the Ford Tri-Motor, a passenger plane of the late 1920s, along with later transport planes such as the Northrop Alpha, the Boeing 247D and the 17,500 pound DC-3, the ancestor of modern airliners.

World War II ushered in the jet age. The museum's collection includes an incredible progression of air-craft. Here are examples of early fighters from the war – such as the German Messerschmitt Me 262, the first jet-propelled warplane used in combat – as well as the planes they begat. The XFD-1 Phantom, designed by the McDonnell Aircraft Corporation in 1946, could fold its wings and take off from and land on an aircraft carrier. The infamous U-2 'spy' plane was developed in the 1950s for high-altitude reconnaissance over the Soviet Union. And along with Chuck Yeager's jet which broke the sound barrier in 1947 is the X-15, a rocket-propelled craft that travelled at 4500 miles per hour, more than six times as fast as Yeager's initial flight. Soaring 67 miles high, at the upper edge of the atmosphere, the ultra-sonic X-15 was a controlled jet that nearly touched outer space.

Space, of course, is where all of these manned flights have led: first out of the atmosphere, then orbiting our planet, and finally to the moon. The artifacts of these spectacular flights are also at the Air and Space Museum: Alan Shepard's *Freedom* 7 capsule, the *Friendship* 7 of John Glenn, the command module *Columbia* which carried Neil Armstrong and crew, a touchable lunar rock, and much of the paraphernalia of lunar landings. The gleaming, mylar-covered *Lunar Module 2* is here, back-up to the Apollo 11 *Eagle* which landed on the moon's surface, along with lunar roving vehicles and space suits.

Above Lindberg's *Spirit of Saint Louis*, pictured when it hung in the Arts and Industries Building of the National Museum.

One glance at the museum's Space Hall shows that many other kinds of missions have taken place beyond our atmosphere. Jupiter, Vanguard, Minuteman and NASA Scout rockets, up to 74 feet tall, reach skyward. There is a back-up of the early *Vanguard I* satellite and a full-scale model of the Tracking and Data Relay Satellite placed in the skies in 1983 by the Space Shuttle *Challenger*. But the enormous Skylab orbital workshop dominates the hall. It is a back-up of a section of the space station launched into orbit in 1973, on which three separate teams of astronauts worked in weightless conditions for as long as 84 days. Visitors can step inside and see how the astronauts lived.

Interlocking, yet completely different in shape and size, are the American and Soviet crafts that duplicate those used in the Apollo-Soyuz test project. Following years of planning, translating and trying to understand each other's technology, scientists from the two superpowers produced ships designed to meet in space. In 1975 the crafts were launched and docking was successfully completed. Astronauts shook hands with cosmonauts, and for two days did experiments together, while sharing meals and cabin space. It was, perhaps, the ultimate in détente, and has been called the world's most expensive handshake, costing $450 million. But it was also a technological triumph and a major step toward future co-operative efforts in space.

Other galleries at NASM look toward the planets and stars. Since the early 1970s, spacecraft have been exploring the planets of our solar system with flyby missions and landings. *Mariner 1* began orbiting Mars in 1971, while two Viking spacecraft descended to the

surface of the red planet in 1975, sending back spectacular photos. Breathtaking images were transmitted
as *Voyager 1* passed by Jupiter in March 1979, revealing
its giant red spot, ring, and four largest moons. In 1981,
it discovered that Saturn was circled by thousands of
rings, while *Voyager 2* sent information on Uranus in
1986. A full-scale test model of Voyager is on display at
NASM, as well as a 1/5 scale model of the Hubble space
telescope launched in 1990 – the largest astronomical
instrument in space.

While governments explore the heavens with the
equipment of highest technology, individuals still continue to pursue their private dreams of flight. Recent
achievements, reminiscent of the earliest days of flying, are stunning in their own right. In 1986, Dick
Rutan and Jeana Yeager circled the globe without refueling in a plane built like a flying fuel tank. This first
non-stop flight around the world was flown at similar
speeds to Lindbergh's voyage in 1928. Another success
comparable to Lindbergh's was the 1978 first Atlantic
crossing by balloon made by Maxie Anderson, Ben
Abruzzo and Larry Newman in their *Double Eagle II*.
And in some ways most extraordinary of all was the
1977 flight of the diaphanous *Gossamer Condor*, the first
sustained, maneuverable *man-powered* flying machine.
Designed by Paul MacCready Jr and piloted by bicy-
clist Bryan Allen using muscle and pedal power, the
70-pound *Gossamer Condor* with its 96-foot wingspan
flew a figure-8 course totalling 1.35 miles. Bird-like, it
seems a successful reminder of the mythological, man-
powered flights of Daedalus and Icarus.

These crafts and many others, now honored in the
National Air and Space Museum, provide an inspiring
visual testimony to the human will, creativity and
courage which have made the most outrageous dreams
come true.

Lilienthal Hang Glider, 1890

This glider hanges in the Flight Test-
ing Gallery on the first floor of the
National Air and Space Museum. Between 1891 and 1896, aviation pioneer
Otto Lilienthal of Germany soared
through the air more than 2000 times
in gliders with birdlike wings and tail
similar to this original Lilienthal
Standard. Shifting his weight by
moving his hips and lower body,
Lilienthal was able partially to control
his craft's direction in the air. Sometimes Lilienthal's glides continued for
several hundreds of feet from the large
hill he had built as a launching pad for
his experiments, before his fragile
craft returned to earth. In 1896 Lilienthal constructed a motor-powered
glider with flapping wing-tips, but
died in a crash before he could test his
craft with its new engine. The Wright
brothers, intrigued by what they read
of Lilienthal's pioneering adventures,
used his research to build their own
early gliders, the precursors of the
first airplane.

Wright Flyer, 1903

Wilbur and Orville Wright's famous flying machine, which changed the course of history, has a place of honor in the National Air and Space Museum's Milestones of Flight Gallery. The Wright brothers had been experimenting with flying machines for years before they constructed this fragile craft in their Dayton, Ohio bicycle shop. The brothers transported their delicate plane by rail to an unobserved site on a beach near Kitty Hawk, North Carolina, which they had chosen because it was known to have the steady wind currents their craft needed to fly successfully. On December 17, 1903, the *Wright Flyer*, with Orville piloting, made the world's first successful powered, manned and controlled flight in a heavier-than-air craft. On the historic first flight, the craft stayed aloft for only 12 seconds and flew a mere 120 feet. By the end of the day the Wrights had made three more flights, the best of which was Wilbur's final effort in which he soared 852 feet in 59 seconds: the future had finally arrived. All that has followed in the history of aviation, up to and including the landing on the moon and the probes to Mars and Venus, had its beginnings in the first flights of Wilbur and Orville Wright.

Spirit of Saint Lous, 1927
(79.763)

In this small, silver Ryan aircraft, the *Spirit of Saint Louis,* Charles Lindbergh became the first person to fly solo non-stop across the Atlantic. The flight from New York to Paris on May 20-21, 1927, lasted 33 hours, 30 minutes and 29.8 seconds and won Lindbergh the coveted $25,000 Orteig prize which New York hotel magnate Raymond Orteig had established in 1919 for the first successful non-stop flight.

Overnight, the slim, 25-year old mail-pilot was an all-American, and perhaps the first international, popular hero. Newspapers around the world carried accounts of the journey, which had been fraught with difficulty. Lindbergh battled against both exhaustion and stormy weather as he flew across the Atlantic, squeezed into his tiny cockpit with a fuel tank blocking his forward vision. When Lindbergh landed in France, a jubilant crowd of 100,000 greeted him at Le Bourget airport outside Paris. The US government responded to Lindbergh's heroic feat by giving him a Congressional Medal of Honor, the first awarded in peacetime. Lindbergh's solo flight stirred public interest in air travel and opened the way to commercial flying.

Amelia Earhart's Lockheed Vega, 1932
(79.763)

In 1932, five years to the day after Lindbergh's historic flight, Amelia Earhart flew solo over the Atlantic from Newfoundland to Ireland, the first woman to cross the Atlantic alone. Earhart made the trip from Newfoundland to Northern Ireland in this red Lockheed Vega in less than 15 hours, combating terrible weather and exhaustion. The journey almost ended in disaster when the Vega's wings iced over and Earhart narrowly avoided crashing into the ocean. Later that year, in the same red Vega, Earhart became the first female aviator to make a solo non-stop flight across the United States, flying from Los Angeles to Newark, New Jersey. In 1937, Earhart undertook her most adventurous flight: around the world in a twin-engined Lockheed Electra. Along with her navigator, Fred Noonan, Earhart disappeared over the Pacific Ocean between New Guinea and Howland Island. For years there were accounts that Earhart had survived and been sighted on one or another isolated Pacific island. To this day, no one knows what became of Amelia Earhart.

Hughes H-1 Racer, 1935
(80.4965)

Although he was best known later in
life as a recluse, Howard Hughes in
the 1930s was a dashing, adventurous
man of many talents. Hughes came to
Hollywood to produce films, but he
was also an inventor with a particular
passion for aviation. He founded the
Hughes Aircraft Corporation, which
became an important defense contrac-
tor during World War II. Not content
merely to build planes, Hughes became a pilot and set a world speed
record in the long-winged cobalt blue
Hughes H-1 racer, considered one of
the most beautiful and graceful planes
ever built. With its highly advanced
design features, the *Hughes H-1* served
as a model for future high-perform-
ance planes.

On September 13, 1935, Hughes
flew his high-tech craft at 353 miles
per hour, a dazzling speed for that
period. Two years later, he set a transcontinental speed record of 7 hours 28
minutes and 25 seconds in the plane. It
was another decade before Hughes's
record was bettered.

Right
Hall of Transportation

The airplanes in the Hall of Air Transportation illustrate the history of
transporting people, mail, and cargo
by air, beginning in the 1920s. The
gallery is crowded with small and
large planes from different eras hanging side by side from the ceiling. The
largest, heaviest – and perhaps most
important – of these planes is the
17,500 pound Douglas DC-3, which
revolutionized air transportation
history. This Eastern Airlines
Douglas DC-3 cruised at 180 mph and
could carry effortlessly a load in ex-
cess of any previously imagined. The
Douglas DC-3 is the prototype for the
commercial airliners which revolutionized travel in the United States.

Near the Douglas DC-3 hang
examples of the early open-cockpit
bi-planes, such as Charles Lindbergh
piloted, which delivered the mail
across the United States. Lindbergh's
1928 transatlantic flight gave a tremendous impetus to commercial flying: the number of passengers in the
United States flown by airlines quad-
rupled that year. Early passenger-
carrying planes included the Northrop Alpha, which held four passengers in an interior cabin at the front of
the plane, and the all-metal Ford Tri-
Motor, which went into service in
1927 and carried twelve to fourteen
passengers who sat on reasonably
comfortable wicker seats. The plane
was said to be built so that it was
'good enough to please Henry Ford
himself.'

Left
Bell X-I, 1947

The Bell XS (X-I) was a joint effort by the US Army Air Forces and the National Advisory Committee for Aeronautics (NACA) in the 1940s. The plane's purpose was simple but previously unimaginable: to fly faster than the speed of sound and break the sound barrier (the invisible shield which caused planes to shudder as they approached it). Unlike many previous aviation feats, which took place in public and won great publicity for the pilot, the Bell X-I was tested secretly in California. On October 14, 1947, test pilot Charles 'Chuck' Yeager broke the sound barrier when he took his Bell X-I, nicknamed the *Glamorous Glennis* for his wife, up to 43,000 feet. Gradually accelerating the Bell's rocket engine, Yeager touched 700 mph and broke the sound barrier. (Mach 1). Amazingly he made this successful and hazardous flight despite a broken rib, an injury he had concealed upon take-off. In time Yeager became legendary for his courage and skill, which was depicted in a novel and film called *The Right Stuff*. Yeager's flight initiated the supersonic age; since then, jets have flown up to Mach 6, six times the speed of sound.

Above
Friendship 7, 1961

In 1961 President John F Kennedy responded to growing concerns about the burgeoning Soviet space program by setting an ambitious goal for the United States: to land a man on the moon before the end of the decade. The first step in the program that ended with the successful Apollo mission in 1969 was the Mercury program of manned spacecraft flights. On February 20, 1962, when Marine Lt. Col. John Glenn became the first American launched into orbit around the globe, 135 million other Americans followed the event on radio and television. Glenn's historic flight from Cape Canaveral (later Cape Kennedy) lasted 4 hours, 55 minutes and took him around the earth three times at a speed of 17,500 mph, to travel a total distance of some 81,000 miles. During Glenn's flight a rocket malfunctioned and he took over manual control of the ship – proving the need to have a trained pilot at the helm. This capsule of the *Friendship 7* craft now on display in the Milestones of Flight gallery was recovered from the Atlantic Ocean off the Bahamas after re-entering the earth's atmosphere.

Left
Space Hall

The theme of the NASM's Space Hall is the hardware that has allowed Americans to travel in space: space boosters, guided missiles, and manned spacecraft. The museum's collection includes Jupiter-C and Vanguard boosters of the sort that launched the first US satellites, including *Exporer I*, America's first successful satellite, which was sent into orbit on February 1st, 1958. The Scout D rocket is an example of the kind used to launch scientific equipment, while the Minuteman III was a US Air Force intercontinental ballistic missile designed to be launched from under-ground silos. All these rockets owe their existence to the pioneering liquid fuel rocket research of Robert H Goddard, funded by a 1917 grant from the Smithsonian, which was the beginning of modern rocketry. A visionary physicist, who taught at Clark University in Worcester, Massachusetts, Goddard predicted as early as 1919 that man would someday reach the moon with rockets. His early experiments with the rockets he built were failures and he was regarded as something of a mad scientist, but in 1926 Goddard launched the world's first liquid-propelled rocket. The exploration of space owes a great deal to Goddard's experiments with liquid-fuel rockets.

Above
Hawker XV-6A Kestrel
(80.13716)

One of the most unusual aircraft on display at NASM is the Hawker XV-6A Kestrel, a jet plane that can lift off vertically from the ground, helicopter-style (also known as a V/STOL, or vertical and short take-off and landing aircraft). A film on view at NASM demonstrates this sci-fi craft in action. First flown on March 7th, 1964, the Kestrel works with a 'vectored thrust' turbo-fan engine. The pilot rotates two sets of nozzles, one of which vectors hot exhaust gases from the turbines, while the other set vectors air from the engine compressor. As a result, the plane can rise up in the air, hover above the ground and then jet off horizontally. When it lands, the craft seems to float back to the ground in a slow vertical descent. The extreme maneuverability of the Hawker Kestrel makes it a useful military aircraft, particularly suited for aircraft carriers.

Left
Lunar Module 2, 1969

'The *Eagle* has landed,' said astronaut Neil Armstrong on July 20th, 1969, on the 4th day, 6th hour, 44th minute and 45th second of the *Apollo 11* moon mission. The *Eagle* was *Apollo 11's* Lunar Module, the first craft to touch down on the moon. Six and a half hours after the Lunar Module carrying Neil Armstrong and Edwin E ('Buzz') Aldrin touched down, 600 million people back on earth watched their television sets as *Eagle's* hatch opened and Armstrong climbed out, making his 'giant step for mankind.' By the time that the Apollo program ended in 1972, a total of twelve astro-

nauts had followed Armstrong in taking a walk on the moon. The Lunar Module 2 on display at NASM was built to be used in an unmanned test flight that was cancelled after the success of the *Apollo 11* mission. Like Lunar Module 1, it has two sections: an ascent and a descent stage. The descent stage, designed to remain on the moon, served as a launch pad when the ascent stage carrying the astronauts rejoined the command module. Although Lunar Module 2 never flew in space, it has been covered with the same glittery aluminized reflecting plastic film that covered Lunar I, to show visitors how the lunar module and its occupants were protected against the fierce heat of the sun.

Above
Lunar Roving Vehicle, 1961

Used as a kind of high-tech dune buggy, *Apollo 15's* Lunar Roving Vehicle (LRV) was the first 'car' to travel over the bumpy, sandy, uncharted surface of the moon. The lightweight *Apollo 15* LRV, powered by two 36-v silver-zinc batteries, weighed just 462 pounds on earth and 76 pounds on the moon. Crawling along its broad, springy tires at a top speed of only eight miles per hour, *Apollo 15's* LRV covered a total of 17.3 miles, allowing astronauts Scott and Irwin greatly increased mobility. The LRVs allowed the astronauts to carry cumbersome, weighty equipment to areas far from their home-base Lunar Modules and to gather soil and rock samples to take back to earth. Three Lunar Roving Vehicles, now out of service, are still on the moon; NASM's LRV was used in tests, but never made the trip to the moon.

Every year millions of Americans, including many school children, visit
the National Air and Space Museum
to learn about the story of flight. The
museum is subdivided into some 25
galleries, each devoted to a single
theme. Most visitors begin with the
Milestones of Flight exhibit, where
the Wright brothers' glider and Lindbergh's *Spirit of Saint Louis* are displayed along with Goddard rockets
and moon rocks. One of the most
popular galleries is the enormous
Space Hall with its sleek, gleaming
rockets, a 16-foot model of the space
shuttle Columbia, and the Skylab
Orbital Workshop. The Orbital
Workshop, which visitors can enter
and walk through, is one of the
museum's most popular exhibits.

Above
Skylab, 1973

NASM's Space Hall is dominated by
the gleaming, 48-foot-long, 80,000
pound Skylab orbital workshop, including a Multiple Docking adapter
and Airlock Module. Like the Lunar
Roving Vehicle, the NASM's Skylab
section never saw service on the
moon, but is a back-up for one which
was launched on May 14th, 1973. The
complete cluster weighed 199,750
pounds and was 118.1 feet long. A
Saturn V rocket propelled Skylab into
space from a gigantic pre-launch
structure the size of a 36-story building. The Skylab, America's first space
station, was used by three different

crews, each consisting of three astronauts. Each crew docked with the
Skylab 'Space Station' in outer space
and manned it on different missions.
While on board Skylab, the astronauts
stayed busy performing a host of
scientific experiments. The first
group spent 28 days aboard the workshop, while the second team more
than doubled that stay, remaining 59
days. The 84-day mission of the third
crew proved the ability of earth-
dwellers to endure weightlessness for
long enough to permit a voyage to
Mars. Visitors by the millions gain a
sense of what it must have been like to
work inside Skylab by stepping inside
the NASM's Skylab back-up in the
Space Hall.

Apollo-Soyuz Test Spacecraft, 1975

Two incongruous shapes creating an asymmetrical form, the American Apollo and Soviet Soyuz crafts join together for a perfect fit. The project began on May 24th, 1972, when President Richard M Nixon and Chairman of the USSR Council of Ministers Aleksei Kosygin established the Apollo-Soyuz test project. The project's goal was the development of a standardized docking system which would be jointly manned by Russian and American astronauts. This made Apollo-Soyuz the first international manned space program and an important step in cooperation in the peaceful exploration of space by the two hostile superpowers. The actual link-up in the sky took place on July 17th, 1975, following years of exchange of knowledge by scientists representing the superpowers. 'Glad to see you,' said Soviet Air Force Colonel Aleksei A Leonov, in English, to US Air Force Brigadier General Thomas P Stafford. The two men shook hands, and over the following two days the Apollo and Soyuz teams lived and worked together. Although a fabulous technological achievement, the cost to the two nations was $450 million and some critics considered it a pricey experiment in détente, while others felt it to be a step toward world peace.

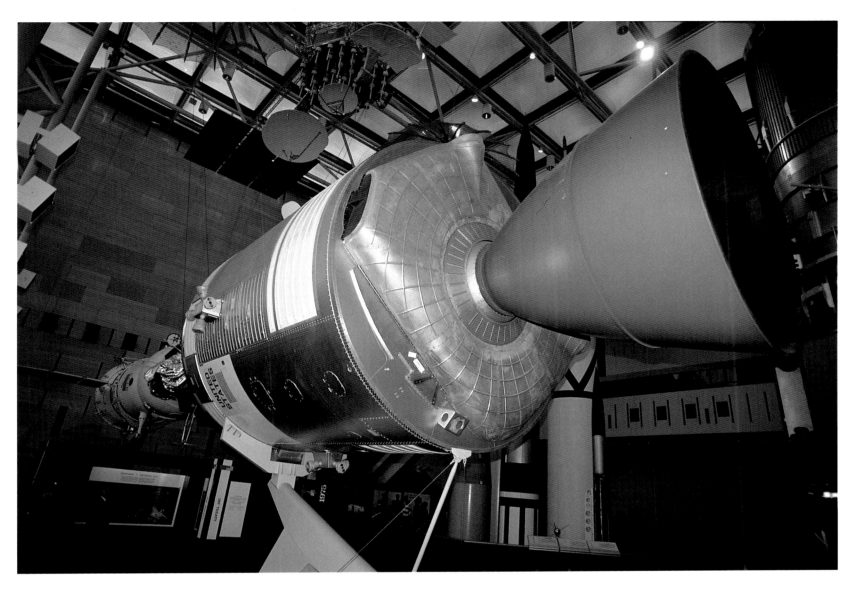

Apollo-Soyuz Test Spacecraft, 1975

The Apollo Command and Service Module has several components: the flared exhaust cone is part of the main propulsion system; the central service module contained the main propulsion system, supplies, and equipment; the pointed command module was home for the astronauts and contained the spacecraft's controls. When the mission was complete, the astronauts returned to earth from space in the command module, abandoning the rest of their craft. During their two days together, the crews of the Apollo-Soyuz mission engaged in a number of scientific experiments. Perhaps their most important breakthrough was the discovery of the first pulsar outside our own galaxy.

Spirit of Texas Bell 206L-1 LongRanger II

The NASM's Vertical Flight Gallery is dominated by rotor-wing helicopters, including the famous *Spirit of Texas*. In 1982, pilots Ross Perot and Jay Coburn flew the *Spirit of Texas*, a Bell 206L-1 LongRanger II helicopter 24,700 miles, over 21 seas and oceans and 26 countries in the first helicopter flight around the world. The flight lasted 29 days, 3 hours and 8 minutes, with lots of stops for refueling. The Vertical Flight Gallery has a number of exhibits on the development of vertical flight, including a reproduction of the great Renaissance artist Leonardo's da Vinci's drawing of a helix, the ancestor of the modern helicopter. It was not until 1907 that Paul Cornu of France actually flew a twin rotor-bladed machine: the first helicopter was airborne for 20 seconds and rose six feet into the air. In 1936 German scientist Dr Heinrich Focke built the first practical double-rotor machine, the Focke-Achgelis FW-61, which could maintain a speed of 76 miles an hour. Intensive research on the helicopter continued because of its obvious military potential as an efficient way to move men and material on the battlefield. In 1942 American citizen Igor Sikorsky's R-4, designed for military use, became the first helicopter in the world to enter production. The original Sikorsky XR-4 (the precursor of the R-4) is on display in the Vertical Flight Gallery.

Voyager, 1986

The unusual design of the Voyager aircraft that hangs in the Milestones of Flight Gallery reflects the fact that it was built as a kind of flying fuel tank. The plane that made the first non-stop flight around the world (December 15th-23rd, 1986) has a central fuel tank and eight storage tanks on each side. Upon take-off, with wings sagging under the weight, it carried 7011.5 pounds of fuel. When the Voyager completed its long journey and landed at Edwards Air Force Base, only 106 pounds of fuel remained. Living in a small, cramped cockpit during the long flight, co-pilots Dick Rutan and Jeana Yeager travelled at speeds similar to Lindbergh's Atlantic crossing in 1928. The two took turns in sleeping as they faced violent thunderstorms and dealt with several mechanical problems: the loss the plane's wing tips, a rear engine oil shortage and fuel pump failure. At one point the engine went dead and they plunged 5000 feet. They arrived tired but safe at Edward Air Force Base on December 23rd, 1986.

CHAPTER THREE

National Museum of American Art

Predating the Smithsonian, the collection that has become the National Museum of American Art was begun by Washingtonian John Varden. In the belief that his young, still muddy and unpolished city required a cultural infusion, Varden set up a public gallery in his home in 1836. The collection moved into the top floor of the then-new Patent Office Building in 1841. A year later, it gained semi-official status as part of the National Institute, sharing galleries with an odd assemblage of exhibits that included stuffed birds, shrunken heads and the original Declaration of Independence. In 1858, the collection became part of the Smithsonian and moved to the recently completed Castle on the Mall, where it was referred to as a 'gallery of art.' It suffered loss and damage in 1865 when a fire devastated the second floor.

During the 1870s, the remaining art works were placed in the Corcoran Gallery and several government buildings for safekeeping and storage. The late nineteenth century was an era of intense scientific and technological interest in the United States, however; the Smithsonian, led by the top scientists and naturalists of the day, focused very little on art, and essentially the collection was forgotten.

Slowly, with the beginning of a new century, this situation began to change. In 1903 Harriet Lane Johnston, President Buchanan's niece, bequeathed a large collection of paintings and sculpture to a 'national gallery of art' which had not yet been created. Spurred by the recent founding of major art museums in New York City, Philadelphia, Boston and San Fransisco, a federal court established the National Gallery of Art in 1906. The growing accumulation of works still did not receive its own building, but was granted a hall in the new National Museum of Natural History when it opened in 1909. And there it remained for many decades, although it was renamed the National Collection of Fine Arts in 1937, when its original title was transferred to Andrew Mellon's collection.

On the final stop of its long journey, the collection returned home again. In 1968, properly displayed for the first time, it was relocated in the Old Patent Office Building; by then, it had gained a wealth of diverse artworks. A dozen years later, it took a new name, the National Museum of American Art.

The building that serves as home to this collection has a colorful history of its own. Approved by Congress as a 'temple of the useful arts,' it was designed to house patent models as well as fine arts. This grand, monumental, Greek Revival structure required several architects and took 30 years to rise from Washington swampland; the first wing of the Patent Office Building was finished in 1840, and the final one in 1867. During the Civil War, with 2000 beds for casualties, it served as a hospital as well as a morgue. Yet gaiety replaced suffering when thousands danced there at President Lincoln's spectacular second inaugural ball in 1865. Walt Whitman, who had often visited the wounded at the Patent Office Building, also attended the President's party. He wrote of the dramatic contrast:

> Tonight, beautiful women, perfumes, the violins' sweetness, the polka and the waltz; then the amputation, the blue face, the groan, the glassy eye of the dying, the clotted rag, the odor of wounds and blood.

Until 1932, the Patent Office displayed its thousands of ingenious and odd American inventions here, but then the building was taken over by the Civil Service Commission. It was partitioned into offices and cubicles and painted in coats of 'government green.' In 1957, a bill before Congress called for demolition to make way for a parking garage. Saved by cries of opposition, the great edifice was turned over to the Smithsonian. Restoration revealed fine details and a mass of marble, including 32 marble pillars supporting the vaulted ceiling of the huge Lincoln Gallery.

The National Museum of American Art now contains 35000 paintings and sculptures and shares the Old Patent Office Building with the National Portrait Gallery and the Archives of American Art. Its exhibits present a panorama covering 250 years of American creativity and including both famous and little-known artists. The collection also serves as an historical and social statement; among its holdings are Colonial portraits, mid-nineteenth-century paintings of the American West, turn-of-the-century portraits, Depression-era government-commissioned WPA (Works Progress Administration) art, and folk art from America's beginnings to the present day.

Early work includes pieces by such artists as Charles

Right The National Museum of American Art, the National Portrait Gallery, and the Archives of American Art share quarters in the Old Patent Office, located between the White House and the Capitol at 8th and G Streets. This handsome Greek-revival building with its courtyard and sculpture garden has a long, varied and distinguished history. Built in 1836-37 to house patent models, it served as a hospital during the Civil War. Abraham Lincoln's second inaugural ball took place in the elegant and spacious second-floor gallery now known as 'The Lincoln Gallery.' The National Museum of American Art includes more than 32,000 works of art, from the eighteenth century to the work of contemporary artists. In addition to its superb collection of paintings, sculpture, engravings and photographs, the museum contains the excellent research library that makes it a world center for research in American art.

Willson Peale, Benjamin West, Raphael Peale, and Gilbert Stuart. Nineteenth-century landscapes and seascapes romanticize America's beauty and grandeur through the works of Thomas Cole, Asher Durand, Winslow Homer, Albert Bierstadt, Thomas Moran and William Holbrook Beard. A collection of 445 paintings of American Indians was created by George Catlin in the mid-nineteenth century over a period of just six years. The artist travelled through the wilderness to 'rescue from oblivion so much of primitive looks and customs as the industry and ardent enthusiasm of one lifetime could accomplish.'

Works by American Impressionists and turn-of-the-century artists feature paintings by Mary Cassatt, William Merritt Chase, Thomas Wilmer Dewing, John Singer Sargent, John H Twachtman, Julian Alden Weir and James McNeill Whistler.

The twentieth-century collections include America's largest group of Federal Art Projects paintings. The Works Progress Administration program had a profound impact on artists, fostering creative goals. The examples here provide a variety of social commentaries that range from despondent reflections on the Depression to idealistic views of labor, industry and American life.

The post-World War II era and the 1950s are represented by painters including Thomas Hart Benton, Andrew Wyeth, Paul Cadmus, and Edward Hopper. A wide range of contemporary art is showcased in the Lincoln Gallery, the splendid 264-foot-long room where dancers promenaded at President Lincoln's inaugural ball. Featured here are sculptures and paintings by artists of such differing visions as Georgia O'Keeffe, Kenneth Noland, Larry Rivers, Helen Frankenthaler, Joseph Cornell, George Segal, Robert Indiana, Clifford Still and Frank Stella.

The National Museum of American Art continues growing and adding to the rich variety of its holdings. In 1974 it broadened its directions by opening the Renwick Gallery as its crafts, design and decorative arts division. The once-forgotten collection has become an important and vibrant part of the Smithsonian.

Above

Mrs James Smith and Grandson,
1775
Charles Willson Peale
Oil on canvas, 36⅜ × 29¼ inches
(92.4 × 74.3 cm)
Gift of Mr and Mrs Wilson Levering
Smith Jr and Museum purchase
(1980.93)

Charles Willson Peale (1741–1827) was
influenced by the work of Boston's
John Singleton Copley and Benjamin
West, whom he met in London.
While Peale painted important historical figures, including George
Washington, many of his portraits
were simply of wealthy colonials. As
a perceptive observer of families, the
artist here captured the love and close-
ness between a grandmother and
grandson, a sensitive painting of
youth joined with the experience of
age. The book on the youth's lap is a
manual of oratory and rhetoric, entitled *The Art of Speaking*, and it is
open at 'Hamlet's Soliloquy.' Peale
founded an important dynasty of
American painters: his sons Rem-
brandt, Raphael and Rubens were the
best known of seventeen artistically
talented offspring.

Bird's Eye View of the Mandan Village, 1832
George Catlin
Oil on canvas, 24⅛ × 29 inches
(62 × 74.2 cm)
Gift of Mrs Joseph Harrison Jr
(1985.66.502)

Beginning in 1830, George Catlin (1796-1872), who had abandoned his law practice to become an artist, spent six years travelling among the American Indians in the west and southwest, painting their vanishing way of life. As Catlin said, 'the history and customs of such a people . . . are themes worthy of the lifetime of one man.' Here the artist captures details showing some of the costumes and ritual objects and the way of life of a tribe that became virtually extinct only years after this painting.

Storm King on the Hudson, 1866
Samuel Colman
Oil on canvas, 32⅛ × 59⅞ inches
(82.2 × 153.2 cm)
Gift of John Gellatly (1929.6.20)

Between about 1825 and 1875 a group of American landscape painters, including Samuel Colman (1832-1920), became known as the Hudson River School of painters. Influenced by the French painter Claude Lorrain, members of the Hudson River School nonetheless developed a distinctly American tone and style. Many paintings were purely landscapes but in others, such as Colman's *Storm King on the Hudson*, the world, here in the guise of different kinds of boats, intrudes on nature. Like many of Colman's paintings, this reveals the artist's coloristic skill: the water and sky glow in silver and gold tones. Storm clouds frequently do cluster in just this way around the peak of Storm King Mountain, close to West Point on the Hudson River. With this natural occurrence as a backdrop, Colman added another dimension: the technological progress of man. Of the three kinds of boats on the water, two – the drifting rowboats and sailboats – are from an earlier and slower time. The steam barges bring modern power into the picture.

While the plumes of dark smoke from the side-wheelers may be seen by modern viewers to pollute the skies, viewer's in Colman's era probably saw the smoke as a sign of progress and of man's ability to tame nature. Man and nature seem not in conflict, but in harmony in this peaceful river scene.

Sleeping Children, 1859
William Henry Rinehard
Marble, 15⅜ × 36¾ × 18¾ inches
(40 × 93 × 47.6 cm)
Gift of Mrs Benjamin H Warden
(1920.4.1)

William Henry Rinehard (1825-1874) was born in Maryland, where he first worked as a sculptor. In his thirties he travelled widely in Europe, studying his craft in Florence and Rome. On his travels, he must often have seen sculptured examples of the sleeping cupids and angels popular in Renaissance art. Those sleeping cupids probably influenced Rinehard when he was given a commission for an important grave monument in 1859. 'I have just finished a group of sleeping children for Sison (sic),' wrote Rinehard in 1859 of the original plaster sculpture, created to produce a marble grave marker for the two children of Hugh and Sarah Sisson in Baltimore. Rinehard showed the children almost as little angels asleep in the long sleep of death, from which, of course, they will awaken at the Resurrection. The original grave monument still stands in Greenmount Cemetery, Baltimore, but severe weathering has virtually obliterated its features. In all, the Sissons lost five children between 1855 and 1864. Death in childhood was commonplace during the nineteenth century and monuments of this sort were enormously popular.

The Sierra Nevada in California, 1868
Albert Bierstadt
Oil on canvas, 72 × 120 inches
(184.3 × 30.2 cm)
Bequest of Helen Huntingdon Hull
(1977.107.1)

Like so many great Americans, Albert Bierstadt (1830-1902), probably the country's best-known landscape painter, was an immigrant. Born in Germany, Bierstadt came to the United States as a toddler but returned to Germany to study painting as a young man. Yet it was the American West that brought forth the fullest expression of his artistic genius. In his best-known paintings, such as *The Rocky Mountains* and *Storm in the Rocky Mountains*, Bierstadt achieves a monumentality that is also obvious in *The Sierra Nevada in*

California seen here. The majestic scope and size of Bierstadt's painting draws the observer into the idealized yet almost photo-realistic setting. The canvas is so large, and the detail so lifesize, that one feels it would almost be possible to step into the scene. Radiant light beams from the center of the painting, where a cloud bank merges with jagged peaks. Interestingly, the mountains which seem so realistic are nowhere to be seen in the Sierra Nevada range: such dramatic peaks are characteristic of the Alps, not of American mountains. The sheer drop of the cliff and the perfect stillness of the mirror-like lake accentuate the drama. Despite the movement of water from the mountains, and geese in flight by the shore, the real motion here seems to be that of the brilliant light that diffuses the painting.

The Grand Canyon of the Yellowstone, 1872
Thomas Moran
Oil on canvas mounted on aluminium,
84 × 144½ inches (215 × 370 cm)
Lent by the US Department of the
Interior, Office of the Secretary
(L.1968.84.1)

Like Albert Bierstadt, Thomas Moran (1837-1926) was an immigrant, born in northern England, who found delight in revealing the awesome grandeur of nature as seen in America's West. Moran seems to have been influenced by the great English landscape painter Joseph Turner, whose works he knew even before he visited England in 1861. Turner's influence is often evident in Moran's interest in depicting light and clouds. Here the canyon is seen from deep within its furrows, which lends it a dramatic mountainous aura. In this panoramic painting, the two human figures on a massive boulder at lower center are dwarfed by the splendid heights of rock above them, as steam erupts from three Yellowstone hot springs. Clearly Moran meant to show man dwarfed by nature. He made the initial sketches for the painting on an exploring expedition to the Yellowstone River in 1871 with Dr Ferdinand V Hayden, and painted the actual canvas when he returned to his New York studio. *The Grand Canyon of the Yellowstone* was widely acclaimed when it was exhibited, and it was influential in moving Congress to declare Yellowstone a National Park. Fittingly, Mt Moran, a towering peak in the neighboring Grand Tetons, is named for the artist who did so much to make the American West alive for his countrymen.

Left
The Lost Balloon, 1882
William Holbrook Beard
Oil on canvas, 47¾ × 33¾ inches
(121.3 × 85.7 cm)
Museum purchase (1922.41.1)

Born in Ohio, William Holbrook Beard (1824-1900) had a studio in Buffalo before settling in New York City in 1861. Along with his less well-known brother James Henry Beard, William Beard gained a reputation for satirical paintings in which human characteristics are attributed to animals. In *Susannah and the Elders*, Susannah is shown as a swan, while the elders are not-so-wise old owls. Many of William Beard's animal paintings were set against landscapes,

as is *The Lost Balloon*, in which nine children and a dog are grouped on a rocky ledge. Above them towers a cathedral rock, its unyielding mass broken by a dark opening, the mouth of a cave or tunnel. All the children watch as a gray hot-air balloon and gondola is perilously blown in the distance, blending with the clouds and barely touched by the rays of the sun. The bank of black clouds threatens to descend, and yet the rays of sun hold promise as they light up the still waters below. Various interpretations of this mysterious painting have been offered, but all tend to suggest that Beard has attempted to convey a sense of human powerlessness, as represented by the children and the lost balloon, in the face of nature's might.

Above
Niagara Falls, 1885
George Inness
Oil on wood, 15⅞ × 24 inches
(40.6 × 61.4 cm)
Gift of John Gellatly (1929.6.67)

Born in New York state, George Inness (1825-1894) fell under the spell of the Barbizon School led by Rousseau and Millet when he studied in France in the 1870s. When he returned to the United States, Inness became one of a handful of artists known as the American Barbizon School, whose paintings were often poetic landscapes. In *Niagara Falls*, Inness shows the broad sweep of the falls and emphasizes the point at which the water meets the cliffs and crashes down with boundless force. A perpetual mist forms as the water from above meets that below. Here, Inness chooses to show the power and grandeur of nature unhindered by man's progress; in later versions (such as *Niagara 1889*, also in the National Museum of American Art) he added smokestacks and factories on the shore.

Right
A Gentlewoman, 1906
Julian Alden Weir
Oil on canvas, 30 × 25 inches
(76.2 × 63.5 cm)
Gift of William T Evans (1909.7.72)

The son of a drawing instructor at the Military Academy at West Point, Julian Alden Weir (1852-1919) studied drawing first in New York and then in Paris. In Paris he fell under the influence of the Impressionists, although his initial reaction was suspicion. To the young Weir, trained in careful draftsmanship, the Impressionists seemed to lack form, but in time Weir himself became known as an American Impressionist. Something of an entrepreneur, Weir advised American art collectors and was an influential figure in the art world. His portrait of *A Gentlewoman* mingles introspection with melancholy and nostalgia, a theme frequently seen in American art at the end of the nineteenth century. The figure is captured at a pensive moment and Weir's coloristic skill is evident in his handling of the filmy dress.

The Caress, 1902
Mary Cassatt
Oil on canvas, 32⅞ × 27⅜ inches
(83.4 × 69.4 cm)
Gift of William T Evans (1911.2.1)

Born in Allegheney City (now Pittsburgh), Pennsylvania, Mary Cassatt (1844-1926) spent almost all her adult life working and studying in Europe. By the early 1870s, her reputation was such that Degas invited her to exhibit her works with the Impresionists. Cassatt was influential in gaining acceptance for the Impressionist movement among American collectors: in 1878 two of her paintings were exhibited at the new Society of American Artists, making them some of the first impressionist paintings shown in America.

In 1892, Cassatt received a major commission to paint a mural of *Modern Women* for the Woman's Building of the World's Columbian Exposition held the next year. Many of Cassatt's finest paintings, including *The Caress* depict domestic scenes, notably tableaux of mother and child; in fact this topic dominated Cassatt's work, especially in her last 25 years. Some critics have suggested that her lifelong study of the many Renaissance paintings on the theme of the Madonna and Child led her to group her subjects in similar poses.

The White Parasol, 1907
Robert Reid
Oil on canvas, 36 × 30 inches
(92.2 × 76.8 cm)
Gift of William T Evans (1909.7.57)

Robert Reid (1863-1929) often painted a woman set among a profusion of flowers; in fact, one critic said that Reid 'cannot see a girl without flowers, and cannot see flowers without seeing a girl.' Trained as an artist in Boston, New York and Paris, Reid worked as a muralist during the 1890s, executing large-scale works for the World's Columbian Exposition of 1893 and the Library of Congress. Along with Childe Hassam, Reid was one of the group of artists known as the 'Ten American Painters' after the sign the ten posted outside their first show in 1898. In *The White Parasol* the pastel coloration of the tiger lilies is influenced by Impressionism. Feminine beauty is idealized as something pale and fragile like the flowers, both needing protection from the harsh light of the sun. All in all, this is less of a portrait than a genre scene that seems to reflect contemporary illustrations of fashions in popular magazines.

Whirligig with Witch and Horse,
1918
Charlie Burnham
Painted metal and wood, 25½ × 25 × 16¼ inches (65.2 × 64 × 41.6 cm)
(1986.65.377)

American folk art has its place in the National Museum of American Art along with paintings and sculpture, although folk art has been valued only relatively recently. Prominent collectors such as Abby Rockefeller were among the first to see the artistic worth of quilts, weathervanes, gaily painted shop signs, and merry-go-round horses. Often folk art has a style that does not seem to change much over time; untutored and un-polished, the designs are often unexpected and quite delightful. Charlie Burnham's *Whirligig with Witch and Horse,* constructed in 1918, is part of the folk art collection of Herbert Waide Hamphill Jr. Burnham, whose exact life dates are unknown, was a sometime-craftsman, hooked rug maker and jack-of-all-trades. His whirligig is made of painted sheet-metal figures including a flying witch, two rotund male figures, a moving horse and an American flag. A propeller-topped water pump, inventively assembled from a faucet and gears, is lowered and raised by the men.

Tanagra (The Builders, New York), 1918
Childe Hassam
Oil on canvas, 58¾ × 58¾ inches
(150.4 × 150.4 cm)
Gift of John Gellatly (1929.6.63)

Behind this apparently simple painting by the American artist Childe
Hassam (1859-1935) lies a fairly com-
plicated story. Tanagra was a city in
ancient Greece; late in the nineteenth
century archaeologists began to un-
earth many distinctive terracotta figu-
rines on the site of Tanagra. Most of
these statuettes depicted elegantly
draped women, and they so caught
the fancy of collectors that many
copies and fakes were sold. Hassam
seems to be making a comment on all
this by posing this American woman,
holding a Tanagra figurine, before a
window in New York where there is
construction going on outside. But as
one of the so-called American Impressionists, Hassam was also particularly
interested in the effects of sunshine on
the interior and the woman, and with
the interplay of colors, moods and
subjects that he introduces he creates a
mystery that transcends the realistic
realm.

Double Portrait of the Artist in Time, 1935
Helen Lundeberg
Oil on masonite, 47¾ × 40 inches
(121.3 × 101.6 cm)
Museum purchase (1978.51)

American artist Helen Lundeberg (1912-), born in Chicago, has spent most of her adult life in California; in addition to her easel paintings, she has done a number of murals for the Federal Arts Project of the Works Progress Administration (1938-42). Her style, which she describes as 'post-surrealist', is well exemplified in this painting, where she has portrayed herself at two stages of life. As a child, she holds a budding flower and rests her hand on a piece of paper or parchment where 'Ages of Man' is dimly written, presumably a reference to Shakespeare's lines; the clock indicates her age, an early hour of time. Linked to the child by an ill-defined slightly ominous shadow – perhaps signifying the insubstantiality of life? – is the artist portrayed as a mature woman, now holding a flower in blossom; in place of the clock is a spherical globe, split and hollow. Clearly loaded with symbols, the painting allows the viewer to interpret it in many ways.

Wild Boars, 1930
Heinz Warneke
Belgian marble, 18¾ × 13¾ × 27 inches
(48 × 33.9 × 69.1 cm)
(1985.6.1)

This work by the German-American
sculpture Heinz Warneke (1895-1983)
is typical of the Art Deco style in
vogue in the 1930s; a stylized rendering that reduces the subject to a rather
tame and decorative piece for aesthetic pleasure. Warneke was born in
Bremen, Germany, and studied there
and in Berlin; after making a name as a
sculptor in Germany he settled in the
USA in the late 1920s; eventually

(1943-68) he served as head of the scul-
pure department at the Corcoran
School of Art and as professor of
sculpture at George Washington University, both in Washington, DC.

Warneke's sculptures, often public
works and usually in stone, can be
seen in many locales, including St
Louis, Philadelphia, the University of
Nebraska, and government buildings
in Washington DC, but his work is
probably best known and most frequently seen at the National Cathedral in Washington DC, where he
carved the clerestory at the south tran-
sept and the *Last Supper* in the tympa-
num over the south portal.

Above right
Dancer and Gazelles, 1916
Paul Manship
Bronze, 32½ × 33 × 10 inches
(82.5 × 84 × 25.5 cm)
Gift of the estate of Paul Manship
(1966.47.8)

The American sculptor Paul Manship
(1885-1966) was a major force in creating the Art Deco style in the United
States. The stylization of natural elements, the ultra-refinement of decorative forms, the echoing of traditional themes: all these are typical of
the Art Deco sculpture at which Manship excelled. Between 1908-12 he
studied in Rome, and his travels to
Greece and around the Mediterranean
reinforced his admiration for ancient
sculpture: a work like this seems to re-
fer to the world of Roman or Greek
bronzes yet was not inspired by any
specific myth. Although Manship's
work no longer excites the critical
praise it once did, one of his sculptures
remains the cynosure of many eyes:
the *Prometheus* in the fountain at the
Rockefeller Center, New York.

Following pages 64-65
People in the Sun, 1960
Edward Hopper
Oil on canvas, 40⅜ × 60⅜ inches
(102.6 × 153.5 cm)
Gift of S C Johnson and Son Inc
(1969.47.61)

Edward Hopper's brand of alienated
realism resulted in haunting paintings
that were almost surreal and often
conveyed the loneliness and isolation
of modern life. Hopper (1882-1967)
worked slowly, usually producing no
more than one or two canvasses each
year. Here no interaction takes place
between individuals sitting close to
each other; proximity produces distance rather than intimacy.

Following pages 66-67
Maquette for Joatinga, 1974
Frank Philip Stella
Oil and lacquer on metal, 35 × 56½ ×
4½ inches (89.6 × 144.6 × 11.5 cm)
Transfer from General Services
Administration (1980.49.15)

Frank Stella (1936-) is one of the leading American painters of the Minimalist School, in which the painting is
conceived as an object. For minimal-
ists, subject is often less important
than technique. Stella is well-known
for his bold use of color and geometric
form, as exemplified here; 'What you
see is what you see,' Stella has said
about his art. Here his three-dimensional brightly painted metal sculpture seems to bridge the gap between
traditional painting and sculpture.
Maquette for Joatinga belongs to Stella's
1974-75 Brazilian series, for which
preliminary drawings were re-drafted
as small maquettes in aluminum and
steel before two largescale versions,
each differently painted, were
executed.

Renwick Gallery

The crafts, design and decorative arts department of the National Museum of American Art is an innovative hybrid known since 1971 as the Renwick Gallery. A consummately modern museum which puts on wildly contemporary shows, it is housed in a French Renaissance building constructed during the Victorian era. The phrase 'Dedicated to Art' is carved in stone high above the entrance to the elaborate structure.

The gallery used to be far more traditional. Designed by James Renwick in 1859 following his success with the Smithsonian Castle, it was to be Washington's first public art museum, the Corcoran Gallery. Set across from the White House on Pennsylvania Avenue, its design boasted a profusion of ornately elegant features: arches and gables, Corinthian columns and pilasters, ornamental plates, cornices, and a mansard roof. Construction came to a halt during the Civil War, and the building was not totally finished until 1874. But President and Mrs Grant spent an evening there in 1871, just a short walk from their stately home, attending a gala preview to raise money for the completion of a landmark-to-be, the Washington Monument.

By 1897 the Corcoran had outgrown its original home and moved on to larger quarters nearby. The empty building it left behind was taken over by the United States Court of Claims and transformed into a functional government processing center whose dedication to art was quickly forgotten and whose architectural style was considered outmoded and unfashionable.

Renwick's charming creation was not rediscovered until it was nearly torn down, well into the twentieth century. In 1965 the Smithsonian reclaimed it just in time and began restoration. Bearing the name of its architect, the old building re-emerged in 1971, colorful, youthful and renovated, as a showcase for American crafts and design.

Yet this modern museum has not forgotten its past.

Preserved in full Victorian splendor is the Grand Salon, a rich and sumptuous room filled with velvet couches, marble-top tables, gaslit statues and Louis XIV-style ballroom chairs. The late nineteenth- and early twentieth-century paintings covering the plum-colored walls are on loan from the National Museum of American Art, while the life-size image of Mr Corcoran, on loan from the private Corcoran Gallery, watches over his old quarters from a prominent position in the salon. Around the corner is the handsome Octagon Room, also beautifully restored to reflect its era.

The main mission of the Renwick, however, is to exhibit works by America's talented crafts and design artists, and it carries out this function with wit and flair. The small permanent collection includes furniture, jewelry, glass and ceramics pieces that are innovative and whimsical, intricate and beautiful and, sometimes, quirky and wild. For example, one exhibit that includes a neo-Art Deco throne chair, delicate hand-blown glass sea shells, and a translucent, finely-crafted wooden bowl also contains one sailfish wall trophy, entirely covered with rhinestones, ping-pong balls, badminton birdies, plastic flamingo drink stirrers and other found objects.

Unlike other Smithsonian museums, the Renwick is best known to the public for its continually changing, highly creative special shows. An exhibition of the works of industrial designer Raymond Loewy featured – along with his new Coke dispenser, Lucky Strike pack and Esso sign – a car in the gallery, a splendidly redesigned Studebaker Avanti. In other shows, visitors have viewed paradoxically non-functional utilitarian objects. A display of craftsmen's images of boats included a boat made out of hay, while a show celebrating the Renwick's tenth anniversary marked the occasion with inedible birthday cakes crafted out of plastic, metal and fabric. An exhibition of American porcelain ranged from fine, modern teacups to china cowboy boots portraying a desert under a starlit sky.

Although still dedicated to art, this museum does not take itself quite as seriously as its Victorian predecessor: in fact, it encourages fun. Never lacking in talent or invention, the Renwick continues to celebrate the new art of a changing world.

Left This entrance leads to the Renwick Gallery, named after the building's architect, James Renwick, who also designed the Castle, the original Smithsonian building. Erected (1859-74) to house the original Corcoran Gallery, in 1972 it was rededicated as a small museum primarily to exhibit American crafts and design works.

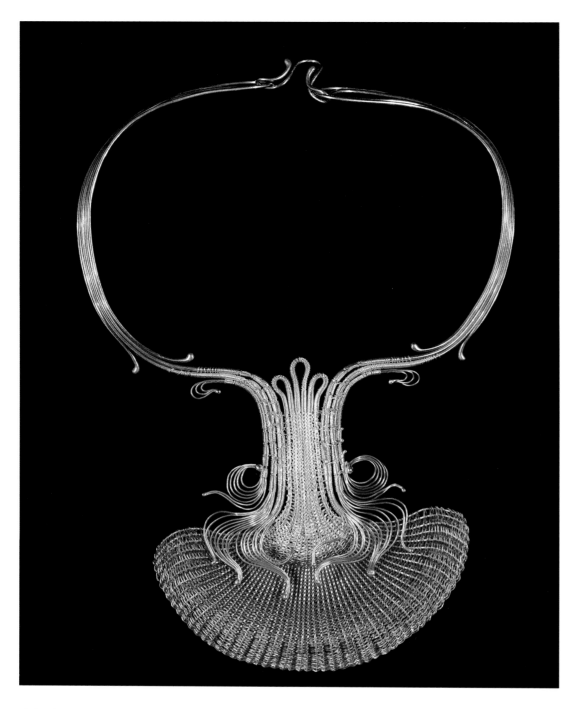

Right
Portal Gates, 1974
Albert Paley
Hand-wrought and forged steel, brass
and copper
Commission for the Renwick Gallery
(1975.117.1)

This is a section of the hand-forged, hot-rolled steel and brass Portal Gates in the Renwick Gallery made by the artist-craftsman Albert Paley, who won the commission from the Renwick in a national design competition in 1972. Since the early 1970s, Paley (born 1944) has been creating hundreds of works – some monumental, some no more than inches high – all from metals such as steel, bronze, brass that he shapes at his vast and busy workshop in Rochester, New York. Bridging the realms of art and crafts, of sculpture and architectural ornamentation, Paley's work also bridges the divide between functional and aesthetic in its appeal; his works may be seen and used by millions of people in locations from hotels to subway stations all over the United States.

Choker # 8, 1978
Mary Lee Hu
Fine and sterling silver, 18 and 24 k gold, lacquered copper, 9¾ × 6½ × 1 inch (25 × 16.9 × 2.56 cm)
Gift of the James Renwick Collectors Alliance (1985.22)

This dramatic neck piece, formerly named Choker # 38, is the work of Mary Lee Hu, an American jeweler. Fine and sterling silver, 18k and 24k gold wires, and brilliantly colored lacquered copper wire have been intertwined, virtually woven together, to create a pattern and texture that is at once simple and dazzling. Mary Lee Hu was born in Lakewood, Ohio in 1943. While she was doing graduate work at Southern Illinois University in 1966, she began to develop her distinctive jewelry by using techniques traditionally associated with textiles. A teacher at the University of Washington since 1980, she enjoys knowing that her jewelry is prized by its many wearers as well as by many museums.

Left
Listening to the East Wind, 1986
Rudi Autio
Stoneware, 39½ × 20 × 24 inches
(101.1 × 51.2 × 61.4 cm)
Gift of James Renwick Alliance and
Museum Purchase through the
Director's Discretionary Fund (1987.30)

Autio makes these distinctive pieces
by shaping the clay and then, while
the clay is still wet, drawing and
painting the image directly on to the
surface. Here the images are horses
and women that Autio has often used
on his ceramic pieces since the 1960s.
Born in Montana in 1926, the son of
Finnish immigrants, he has taught
since 1956 at the School of Fine Arts at
the University of Montana.

Right above
Throne Chair, 1924
Robert Whitley
Curly maple/walnut, 34½ × 36 ×
26 inches (88.3 × 92.1 × 66.6 cm)
Gift of Mr Bradford McCormick
(1986.36)

This Throne Chair, although it
derives from a traditional Windsor
chair, bears the mark of contemporary Pennsylvania cabinetmaker
Robert Whitley's creative hand. The
son and grandson of cabinetmakers,
Whitley is noted both for his original
designs and for his ability to repro-
duce antique furniture.

Right below
Untitled, 1982
Dale Chihuly
Glass, 7½ × 24 × 18 inches (19.2 × 61.4
× 46.1 cm)
Gift of Milton C Bickford (1983.111)

This untitled piece is a work from his
'Sea Form Series' by the most cele-
brated contemporary American
artist-craftsman working with blown
glass. In 1971 Chihuly established the
Pilchuck Glass Center north of
Seattle, which quickly became the
moving force in reviving modern art
glass in the United States. Chihuly's
own work has gone through many
phases as he pushes the art and craft of
blowing glass to the limits in terms of
colors, shapes, textures and expres-
siveness.

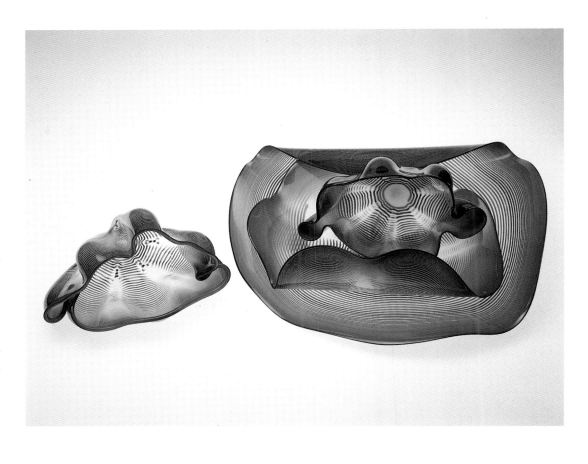

Chapter Four

National Museum of American History

The name of the National Museum of American History is basic and straightforward. Someone who has not visited it might picture within things that are old, genealogical, and of course 'historical': items to do with the *Mayflower*, rows of Revolutionary and Civil War uniforms, yellowed documents preserved in glass display cases. But this museum belies its name; it is a fascinating place where the past meets the present, and it puts on quite a show.

Inside the entrance hangs a gigantic American flag, with stars representing the 15 states that constituted the nation in 1814. It is in fact a *painting* of a flag, shielding and protecting the fragile historical treasure that lies behind it: the actual star-spangled banner seen by Francis Scott Key during the War of 1812, which inspired him to write the American national anthem, *The Star Spangled Banner*. Every hour on the half hour the anthem is heard in the background, and the huge painting is briefly lowered to reveal the genuine article behind it.

Near the flag the 240-pound brass bob of the Foucault pendulum swings back and forth, knocking down small pins at regular intervals. French physicist Jean Bernard Léon Foucault invented the prototype for this device in 1851, to demonstrate that the earth rotates on its axis. The watcher's eye is fooled into perceiving a clockwise rotation of the pendulum, which really remains constant as the earth rotates counterclockwise.

On the ground floor, the chugging of a steam engine slowly building up speed indicates a room filled with colorful vintage locomotives. Inside Railroad Hall the source of the sound is a colossal green engine, Locomotive 1401, built in 1926 and weighing in at 561,600 pounds. It was rolled through Washington on temporary tracks and through an open wall of the museum two years before the structure was completed.

Of course it is understandable that a powerful American railroad and a grand historic flag might serve as centerpieces to a museum focusing on American history. But why a mid-nineteenth century mechanism invented by a Frenchman?

Invention, technology and industry have profoundly affected and sometimes defined the American way of life, as was reflected in the museum's original name, the Museum of History and Technology. Built in 1964, the massive marble building took over exhibits from the old Arts and Industries Building which had been accumulating for many decades. It was designed to be substantial and utilitarian: a museum that could comfortably house and exhibit trains, automobiles and large machinery along with myriad smaller artifacts from American history. The name was changed in 1980 to encompass a broader scope of interests, but technology still makes an impressive showing here.

There is, however, no assumption that American inventiveness, technology and creativity were born in isolation. The museum recognizes the importance of such foreign inventors as Jean Foucault; it proudly displays a 1701 violoncello made by the Italian master Antonio Stradivari; and it exhibits the printing press from London on which Ben Franklin is said to have worked as a journeyman. The displays of inventions, and their progeny, take the visitor on a progression through time, showing the machines that irreversibly changed human lives. Here is Elias Howe's first difficult-to-use sewing machine side-by-side with Singer's patent model, the true forerunner of the machine used today. Here are Whitney's cotton gin, Morse's tele-

Left The National Museum of American History, located on the Mall, began its existence in 1858 as the Museum of History and Technology.

graph, Bell's first telephone, Edison's recording machines, Ford's Model T. We see how the 1826 camera of Joseph Nicéphore Niepce of France evolved into high-tech photography, and how early motion pictures begat today's multi-billion dollar entertainment industry. Wonderful, antiquated, mechanical oddities abound: an 1890 stereopticon – a magic lantern capable of projecting three images at once; an 1865 'writing ball', the forerunner of the typewriter; an 1870 hat-brim shaper. Here are early telescopes and microscopes, radios and televisions. Gaily-painted horse-drawn carriages and stagecoaches of the nineteenth century evolve into the twentieth century's bright, horseless carriages with handcranks and kerosene tail-lights, and then to automobiles, trucks, buses, and tractors.

Time itself is represented by an array of clocks, including a model of the 1350 astronomical clock of Italian inventor Giovanni de' Dondi. Also here is the 13-foot-high Great Historical Clock of America, with its representations of the Pilgrim Fathers landing at Plymouth Rock, Paul Revere taking his famous ride, a procession of revolving presidents, and a large, immobile Statue of Liberty.

But the history of a nation, even so young a nation as the United States, is composed of countless pieces. The Museum of American History holds an incredible proportion of these parts; it has more than 18 million objects in its collection. Sports fans might catch a look at a ticket booth from Yankee Stadium. Or a thrilling variety of gloves which once covered the hands of champs: the red autographed pair worn by Muhammad Ali when he won his world heavyweight title; Sandy Kaufax's baseball glove; and Bobby Orr's hockey gloves. Philatelists can find one of the rarest, most valuable stamps in the world: a 24-cent airmail stamp from 1918 which was accidentally printed with its picture of a biplane upside down. Political buffs will see a tremendous collection of presidential campaign memorabilia dating back to George Washington's time, along with the inaugural ball gowns of our First Ladies. And a new generation of computer operators, adults and children alike, can learn how our 'Information Age' evolved, and then enjoy some hands-on play using futuristic software and hardware.

Items of Americana are represented in charming collections of folk art. Turn-of-the-century wooden carousel animals include not only horses and lions, but such unusual carved creatures as a stork and, sea monster. A great dolls' house, the home of Mr and Mrs Peter Doll, contains more than 20 rooms filled with early twentieth-century miniature period furnishings. Tobacco-store Indians compete for attention with the wooden figures which attracted customers to late-nineteenth-century dressmakers, tailors and toyshops. Other art collectables feature Tiffany glass, quilts, pottery and ceramics.

The evolution of medicine is demonstrated by complete shops, dental and medical offices and laboratories. An eighteenth-century European apothecary, with an alligator and a tortoise hanging from the ceiling, leads the way to a 'modern' 1890s American drugstore with patented medicines, cosmetics – and leeches. A 1905 bacteriological laboratory is here, along with a modern computerized room that contains the first whole-body CAT scanner. Fearsome-looking antique surgical equipment gives way to a contemporary hospital operating room.

But the reality of America's history must also include a recounting of social and political antagonisms, hardships and suffering. As a nation that has gone to war many times, America's story includes persecution, bigotry and violence. The Museum of American History puts a harsh spotlight on some of the shameful episodes: the slavery and persecution of Afro-Americans; the internment of Japanese-Americans in camps during World War II; the struggle of women for equal rights.

Elsewhere the museum shows a lighter side of history. A display devoted to US chiefs of state can overlook political achievements and focus instead on presidential toys, such as Teddy Roosevelt's original teddy bear. Show business is here too: onlookers can hardly help but feel star-struck when standing inches away from the magical ruby slippers worn by Judy Garland in *The Wizard of Oz* (even though the 'rubies' are really red sequins). What are puppets Howdy Dowdy, Kermit the Frog and Charlie McCarthy doing in a national museum? And why are C3PO and R2D2 from *Star Wars* included in an exhibit of *real* robots and computers?

And of course music is part of America's heritage. An outstanding group of musical instruments includes not only home-made American banjos, folk violins and dulcimers, but also stringed instruments created by Italian masters, along with magnificent woodwinds, harpsicords, and pianos. The instruments are not simply there for display; musicians play them regularly, giving concerts of classical, romantic and baroque music.

Left Back in the 1930s, this is how the museum displayed its collection of vintage automobiles. Many of these vehicles, including the first car to go a mile a minute and examples of the venerable Hayes and Duryea models of 1893, may still be seen but they are now displayed in a far more attractive manner.

Right This light family coach, pictured when it was donated to the Smithsonian in 1931, dates to the period of the American Revolution. It may have belonged to George Washington and been used by him at Mount Vernon. That makes this well-preserved vehicle one of the oldest known surviving carriages made in the United States.

Right
Harpsichord, 1770
Jean-Marie Dedeban, Paris

The collection of musical instruments at the Museum of American History includes American folk instruments such as banjos and dulcimers as well as rare eighteenth and nineteenth century instruments, such as this harpsichord made in 1770 in Paris. Harpsichords are keyboard instruments with two or more strings to a note, which are plucked by jacks or quills. In the nineteenth century, pianos replaced harpsichords for general use. Restored to playing condition, the Smithsonian harpsichords are heard in concerts given at the museum.

Above
Benjamin Franklin's Printing Press, 1726

In the mid-1770s, the eminent American statesman and scientist Benjamin Franklin entered the Watts printing shop in London and declared that he had practiced his early craft on this wooden press when he worked as a journeyman printer in London from 1725-26. In the forty years that had passed, Franklin had become one of the most successful publishers in the colonies and was also known as an inventor. Franklin's London press was presented to the United States by the British in 1841.

Continental Gondola 'Philadelphia', 1776

The *Philadelphia*, the oldest existing American man-of-war gunboat (known at the time as a 'gondelow' or 'gondola'), was part of an eight-boat flotilla that fought under Brigadier General Benedict Arnold during the Revolutionary War. The 54-foot long oaken vessel was launched on Lake Champlain in August 1776. On October 11th, following a six-hour fight against British forces under Sir Guy Carleton, the *Philadelphia* and her crew of 44 went down off Valcour Island in Lake Champlain. Although General Arnold lost the battle, he managed to thwart the critical British attack on Fort Ticonderoga. In 1935, the *Philadelphia* was raised from the bottom of Lake Champlain with its 12-pounder gun still in its original slide carriage. The 24-pounder cannon shot and the hole that sank her are visible in the ship's starboard bow.

Concord Coach, 1848

This gaily-painted six-passenger coach was built in the Lewis Downing coach shops in Concord, New Hampshire in 1848; hence its name. The Concord Coach was used to convey passengers back and forth between the train station and local hotels. Appropriately, the coach's capacious design allowed a large amount of baggage to be held on the rooftop, below the driver's seat and on the rear rack. Coaches similar to this one were exported from Concord around the world, to remote areas of South America, Africa, and Australia. The standard mail coach, which carried mail and passengers to areas where the trains did not run, were larger versions of the Concord coach. The spread of the railroad and the invention of the automobile were the death knell for the coach industry and many skilled workers who had crafted and decorated these vehicles had to find new jobs. This Concord Coach was a gift to the Smithsonian from the great American humorist Will Rogers, and Fred Stone.

Engine 1401, 1926

This enormous, bright green passenger engine, the 1401, is the centerpiece of Railroad Hall. Visitors are attracted by its sheer bulk as well as by the amplified sounds of an engine building up speed that seem to make the mighty creature come alive. Built in 1926 for the Southern Railway, the 12-wheel PS 4 Pacific engine together with its tender weights 561,600 pounds and is nearly 92 feet long. It was able to pull up to 14 steel cars weighing some 800 tons at a cruising speed of 80 mph. For most of its career, this engine travelled the rails in the Carolinas, covering some two million miles in all before it was taken out of service toward the end of the steam era in 1951. In 1945, the 1401 performed a solemn duty: it was one of the ten locomotives that hauled Franklin D Roosevelt's funeral train from Georgia to Washington DC. In 1961, the train travelled through the streets of Washington on a temporary track to the Museum of American History. It was rolled in through a window opening two years before the museum was completed, and stored until going on permanent display.

Carousel Horse

Many festive carousels were built in the later nineteenth century. Sculptures in motion offering a ride set to music, these mechanical pleasures were found at carnivals, country fairs and ocean resorts. Some early carousels were circular platforms on which all animals were stationary, without poles or vertical motion. Carousel animals combined realistic and fanciful elements. While often considered folk art, some of these charming beasts were carved by trained sculptors.

The Dentzel family of Germantown, Pennsylvania, was particularly acclaimed for the grace and beauty of its carousel animals, all of which were gaily painted. In addition to the horse, the most common carousel creature, the Smithsonian's collection includes a lion, zebra, giraffe, stork and rare sea monster. The Institution celebrates the old-fashioned joys of summer each year by offering rides on a working carousel in the Mall.

Sitting in these homey pieces of furniture in their working-class house in Queens, New York, Archie and Edith Bunker (played by Carroll O'Connor and Edith Stapleton) were seen – by virtually all of America – talking, squabbling and debating about personal and political issues in the enormously popular television show *All in the Family*. The show ran from 1971 to 1979, and the Bunkers broke down the previous television tradition of only showing happy families, living free from everyday strife. With humor and poignancy, *All in the Family* faced prejudice and other social issues head on, bringing a dose of reality into American entertainment.

Right below
Ruby Slippers, 1939

Judy Garland won the hearts of her contemporaries – and the hearts of generations of Americans to come – by singing 'Somewhere Over the Rainbow' in the 1939 film *The Wizard of Oz*. As Dorothy, she trekked from Munchkinland to The Emerald City in these magical ruby slippers and shared adventures with her new friends, the Scarecrow, the Tin Man and the Cowardly Lion. The shoes are actually one of several pairs used in the production of the movie, while the 'rubies' are red sequins. In Frank Baum's original children's book, the slippers were silver but, thanks to Judy Garland, they will always be remembered as the ruby slippers.

Above
Lucy Stone's Suffrage Wagon

Lucy Stone was one of the leaders of the women's rights movement of the nineteenth century. Stone founded the *Women's Journal*, the official voice of the National American Women's Suffrage Association, in 1870 and toured the country with her suffrage wagon trying to convince her fellow citizens that women should have the vote. The bright yellow wagon was covered with attention-grabbing slogans and carried flyers, buttons, and literature on the women's movement. The wagon reads 'Vote Yes on Amendment Number 1 on Election day. All areas pertaining to the home are woman's business as well as man's. Women need the vote.' The whole display is a tribute to a tireless pioneer.

Left
The Star-Spangled Banner, 1812

Francis Scott Key saw this tremendous flag raised defiantly against the British at sunrise and was inspired to jot down part of a poem beginning, 'O, say can you see/By the dawn's early light.' Ironically, when Key's poem was printed it was set to an old English drinking song, 'To Anacreon in Heaven.' During the Civil War the song gained popularity, but it was not until 1931 that Congress designated it the national anthem. Because of the flag's fragility, it now hangs under a protective covering: a giant painting of a flag. Every hour on the half hour, the painting is lowered so viewers may see the original Star-Spangled Banner, as the national anthem plays in the background.

Left above
American Racing Cars

Racing cars seem to have appealed to Americans from the earliest days of motor vehicles. The museum's collection includes everything from a 1903 Bullet No. 2 that could travel at 84 mph to sleek monsters that have raced at Daytona and in the Indy 500.

Above
First Ladies

The museum's extensive collection of clothing provides a glimpse of changing fashions throughout the history of the United States. You can see everything from modest black wool swimsuits of the 1920s to the first daring bikinis of the 1960s. One of the most popular exhibits is the collection of dresses worn by America's First Ladies, beginning with Martha Custis Washington. It is not just an interest in changing styles and fashions that makes this exhibit so popular; many visitors sense that some insight may be gleaned into the personalities of the women from their important choice of an inaugural gown. Whether they remain in the background of their husband's administration or become actively involved, our First Ladies become celebrities of the land and gain star qualities. Here, Rosalynn Carter and Betty Ford wear the simple but elegant gowns they danced in at their husbands' inaugural balls.

Arts and Industries Building

The Arts and Industries Building, originally called the National Museum, was built to display the trainload of modern wonders that arrived in Washington when the gala 1876 Philadelphia Centennial Exposition closed. When completed in 1881, the elaborate structure designed by Adolph Cluss hosted President Garfield's inaugural ball. At the time, it was considered a model museum. Built in the shape of a cross with a central rotunda, it had lots of airy space for exhibits and plenty of natural light. Despite a profusion of colorful, ornate Victorian touches, it cost only three dollars per square foot to construct; the least expensive building ever erected by the government in Washington.

For many years the Smithsonian's natural history collection was housed here, before moving to the new Museum of Natural History in 1911. Over time the Arts and Industries Building became the 'nation's attic,' holding anything and everything, from First Ladies' gowns, coins and stamps, guns and swords, Alexander Graham Bell's original telephone and artificial teeth, to Brunnhilde, the transparent woman whose internal organs lit up every 15 minutes as a recorded lecture explained their various functions.

For a long time, aircraft were hung from the industrial iron ceiling of the Arts and Industries Building. The *Spirit of St Louis* made its home there, and Charles Lindbergh used to come after hours, when he was working on his autobiography, to contemplate the small plane that had helped make him a hero. During the 1960s towering rockets, an incongruous sight, stood guard outside the old Victorian building.

Eventually the miscellaneous collections and the aviation displays moved in to two new Smithsonian museums, and the venerable Arts and Industries Building was designated office space. As the nation's bicentennial approached, however, it was decided to restore it to its original purpose and recreate the year 1876. Where other museums were concerned with modernizing their displays and keeping up with new trends, this one decided to grow old. First, however, it had to be freshened up a bit. Inside it was re-painted, re-stenciled and re-tiled. Huge flags were draped and brightly-colored machinery was rolled in, along with vintage trains and artifacts.

The museum took on a celebratory feeling, proudly displaying all manner of strange and wonderful American products that were either actually shown at the Philadelphia Centennial or else suited the period; antique signs were recreated to help advertise goods and wares. The Arts and Industries Building grew cluttered once more, this time with century-old, gaily-painted mechanical objects: printing presses, machine tools, cannons and a massive, 19-ton refrigeration compressor. Totem poles from the Centennial's Indian

exhibition were hauled in, along with a 45-foot model of a naval steam sloop-of-war, buggies and delivery wagons, a giant pipe organ and a life-sized plaster camel. Old glass and mahogany display cases were used to exhibit in authentic fashion some of the smaller items, such as French lace, homeopathic supplies, telescopes, guns and clocks, as they would have appeared 100 years earlier. And small, cramped booths repre-

senting the states were filled with such items as the coat of that famous Illinois son, Abraham Lincoln, and Iowa husks of corn.

Newly furnished in old attire, the 1876 exhibition in the Arts and Industries Building re-opened for the nation's 1976 bicentennial, inviting visitors to step back in time as they passed through the door. The odd hodge-podge feeling of the place has been delighting

Above The second oldest of the Smithsonian buildings, the Arts and Industries Building opened its doors in 1881.

people ever since. This exuberant old museum will be going through another change again soon, and will focus on yet another novel and exciting aspect of the Smithsonian's collections.

Nautical Display

The history of transportation has a prominent place in the collection of Arts and Industries Building. Until the Air and Space Museum was opened, the nation's collection of airplanes was housed here. This is one of the first museums in which heavy objects, such as airplanes, were displayed by being hung from the ceiling – to the considerable consternation of visitors, who wondered if they could come loose from their moorings and crash to the floor! Today, the museum has an extensive collection of models to illustrate nautical history. One of the museum's great exhibition rooms is crowded with models, including the 312-foor steam sloop of war *Antietam*, the 1916 cargo schooner *CC Mengel Jr.,* the steam frigate *Mississippi*, and the famed 44-gun *Old Ironsides*, which fought during the War of 1812. Commercial shipping of the twentieth century is shown through models of freighters dating from 1919 to 1971. Other nautical exhibits feature propellers, buoys, engines and scrimshaw objects.

Morse Electro-Magnetic Telegraph Exhibit

Samuel B Morse studied the French physicist André Marie Ampère's ideas about electrical current and worked with other scientists, including Joseph Henry, the first Secretary of the Smithsonian, to devise an electric telegraph. In 1844, after more than twelve years of intensive research and experiments, Morse transmitted the message 'What hath God wrought' over a wire running from Washington to Baltimore. At once, Congress realized the invention's amazing potential; all too soon, during the ter-rible years of the Civil War, the telegraph using 'Morse code' was to become a vital means of rapid communication. The Arts and Industries Building's exhibit of Morse's electromagnetic telegraph, like so many of the museum's exhibits, was originally displayed in the Philadelphia Centennial of 1876. Morse was an exceptionally talented inventor who introduced the daguerreotype camera to America and worked on submarine cable telegraphy. He was also an able and accomplished artist: he gained a considerable reputation as a portrait painter and founded the National Academy of Design.

Right
Baldwin Locomotive 'Jupiter',
1876

The *Jupiter*, engine number 3, was manufactured by the Baldwin Locomotive Works in 1876. This wood-burning, 8-wheel 36-gauge passenger engine travelled at speeds of 25–40 mph. The prominent red, wedge-shaped cowcatcher at the front of the engine cleared the tracks of obstructions. The *Jupiter* stayed in service until the 1950s, ending its travels in Guatemala. An 1870s company sign on display with the locomotive declares that the Baldwin Works is the 'Oldest Active Manufacturer of Locomotives in America,' and boasts that it 'employs nearly 2,000 hands when times are good and is one of the great business houses in our industrial nation.'

Boericke and Tafel Medicinal Publishers Homeopathic Exhibit

The nineteenth-century German physician Samuel Hahnemann is regarded as the founder of homeopathy, a system which calls for the use of minute doses of drugs to produce the symptoms of a disease, setting the body's defenses in motion. Hahnemann's ideas were sufficiently popular in the United States that the Hahnemann Medical College and Hospital was founded in Philadelphia in 1848. The Arts and Industries Building's collection includes this display on the Boericke and Tafel Company of San Francisco, New York and Chicago, which served both as homeopathic pharmacists and medical publishers. The display of their wares includes books such as *The Homeopathic Family Guide* and *A Manual of Pharmacodynamics*, along with bottles and vials of drugs, 'therapeutics of nervous diseases.' The Smithsonian's collection of medical paraphernalia reflects hundreds of years of experimentation and breakthrough in the field of medicine.

Right
Babcock and Wilcox Patent Water-Tube Steam Boiler

This is a cut-away model of one of the early Babcock and Wilcox water-tube steam boilers that helped to revolutionize the great age of steam, thus advancing the second phase of the Industrial Revolution. Steam boilers had come into use by the end of the eighteenth century and were soon powering ships, locomotives, mills and factories, but there was an increasing demand for more and more steam and at higher pressures than the standard fire-tube boilers could produce. In 1867 two British engineer-inventors, George H Babcock and Stephen Wilcox, patented the first successful water-tube boiler: water moved through the tubes, was heated by the surrounding fire and gases, and then, expanded some 1600 times in volume, came off under great pressure as steam in a collecting 'drum' above. Although improvements were introduced over the years, steam boilers based on this principle met the needs of industry and society for the next sixty years.

CHAPTER FIVE

Freer Gallery

The unlikely friendship that developed between the reserved Detroit industrialist, Charles Lang Freer, and the flamboyant, hot-tempered, expatriate American artist James McNeill Whistler is the true foundation of the Freer Gallery. The contents of the Gallery create a similarly unlikely match; the main body of the collection combines thousands of delicate and exquisite Asian masterpieces with the works of Whistler.

Charles Freer lived out the American dream. As a boy from a family of little means, he dropped out of school at the age of 14 to go to work in a factory. He moved on to a railroad job, worked hard, was noticed for his ambition and talent, and rose rapidly to success in the business of manufacturing railroad cars. By the time he was 46 years old, Freer had arranged a stunning merger of 13 railroad car companies and retired with a vast fortune.

Along the way, the industrialist had become a self-taught connoisseur of art. A group of European etchings was the start of his collection, but more important to him was the acquisition of his first set of etchings by Whistler in 1887. 'My purchasing began the day thereafter and has continued ever since,' he once said.

In 1890, on Freer's first trip to Europe, he met Whistler in London. The businessman asked the artist for advice on collecting, and Whistler – himself influenced by the arts of the Orient – urged Freer to study Oriental culture and purchase pieces from China and Japan. Freer took the advice. From 1895 to 1911, he traveled through Europe, Japan, China, Java, India, Ceylon, Egypt and the Near East, searching for the finest objects he could find, and brought back with him enough ancient treasures to fill a museum. These rare works of art included paintings, ritual bronze vessels, porcelains, jades, cloisonné and lacquer objects, sculptures, and gold and silver metalwork.

During the period of his acquisition of Oriental arts, Freer's acquaintance with Whistler grew into friendship and patronage. Gradually he amassed over 1200 paintings, etchings, prints and objects by the artist, including works inspired by Oriental compositions, muted seascapes and impressionist oil paintings of women. He also purchased about 200 works by other contemporary American painters including Winslow Homer, Thomas Dewing, John Singer Sargent and Abbott H. Thayer.

In 1904 he offered his collection to the Smithsonian, along with funds to build a museum to house it. The gift was accepted by Congress in 1906, with a provision that permitted Freer to keep the collection until his death, at which time it would be placed in a new building on the Mall. Freer's gift totaled 15,434 objects, including 1473 works in the American section. The terms of the gift set some firm limits, however: no objects from the collection could be loaned to other museums; nor could artwork from other collections be exhibited. An endowment allowed for the acquisition of Asian artworks of highest quality, but no further additions could be made to the American collection.

Freer worked closely with New York architect Charles Platt on the plans for an elegant yet modestly sized building in the style of a Florentine Renaissance palace. Its two-story design has a philosophical purpose as much as an architectural one: built for exhibition and study, the museum is meant to foster the appreciation of art on both an intellectual and an aesthetic level. A central courtyard offers visitors a quiet spot to consider the relationship between art and nature, an important concept to Freer. When the building opened to the public in 1923, three years after Freer's death, peacocks were released to stride about the courtyard.

This was a fitting touch, for among the graceful and delicate porcelains and paintings of the East displayed in the Freer are many depictions of exotic birds, including colorful songbirds, cranes and a phoenix as well as peacocks. Echoing and embellishing this theme is a room which is considered one of the great treasures of the Smithsonian: Whistler's fabulous Peacock Room. A dining room ornamented with a mock-feather sculpted ceiling, gold-leaf peacocks and turquoise and gilded leather paneled walls, the Peacock Room was created in the London home of shipping magnate Frederick R Leyland. Excessive? Leyland certainly thought so. He was out of the country when Whistler radically remodeled the room without his knowledge, and when he returned he threw the artist out. Nonetheless, he kept everything exactly as Whistler created it. Eventually the room was sold to Charles Freer, dismantled, reassembled and shipped to Detroit. Later, it was set up once again in the museum that carries Freer's name.

Above The Freer Gallery, built with funds provided by the Detroit industrialist Charles Lang Freer, was designed by the architect Charles Platt in the style of a Florentine Renaissance palace. It was opened to the public in 1923 .

Left Entitled *Rose and Silver: Portrait of Mrs Whibley,* this portrait from the early 1890s by James NcNeill Whistler is of his sister-in-law, Ethel Birnie Philip. Before she married Charles Webley in 1894, she was Whistler's secretary and model. This is an unusual work, a full portrait in watercolor; possibly it is a study for one of the several oil portraits Whistler subsequently painted of this obviously charming woman. (Watercolor on paper, 11⅛ × 7⅜ inches, 28.5 × 18.9 cm)

The Freer is not a large museum, when compared with some of its neighbors. A significant portion of its space is devoted to research and study, at the direction and bequest of its founder. While its holdings now number about 26000 works of art, only a small fraction of these may be displayed any time.

Still, there is much beauty to be found here; the Freer's Oriental collection is considered one of the finest outside Asia. The museum itself has been termed 'small but perfect.' It is a refined perfection, created mostly in ancient times by distant cultures yet shaped, as a whole, by one self-educated man.

Arrangement in Black and White,
c.1876
James McNeill Whistler
Oil on canvas, 76½ × 36³⁄₁₀ inches,
(195.8 × 92.9 cm)
(04.78)

Despite its abstract-aesthetic title, this
is a portrait of Maud Franklin,
Whistler's model and mistress for a
decade. Although they never married, she referred to herself as 'Mrs
Whistler.' Whistler's painting captures both the elegance and the pert-
ness of a self-assured young woman.
For a time, the work was mistakenly
called *L'Americaine,* although Franklin was in fact British. Charles Freer
engaged in lengthy negotiations with
its original owner to obtain this portrait, one of the most prized in his collection of 1270 Whistler works.

**Nocturne: Grand Canal,
Amsterdam,** 1883–84
James McNeill Whistler
Watercolor on paper, 8^{15}⁄₁₆ × 11^{3}⁄₁₆
inches, (22.9 × 28.5 cm)
(02.161)

This is one of a series of four water-color 'Nocturnes' of Amsterdam, a title suggested by Whistler's one-time patron, the British shipping magnate Frederick Leyland. Whistler wrote to Leyland: 'I can't thank you too much for the name 'Nocturne' as a title for my moonlights. You have no idea what an irritation it proves to the critics and consequently pleasure to me – besides, it is really charming and does so poetically say all I want to say and no more than I wish.' Quite daring in his technique, Whistler blends several washes of dark colors to create the effect of a foggy evening, with indistinct anonymous figures in the foreground and the illuminated houses reflected on the canal.

Above

The Peacock Room, 1876-77
James McNeill Whistler
Oil color and gold on leather and
wood, 167⅞ × 398 × 279½ inches,
(429.6 × 1018.8 × 715.5 cm)
(04.61)

Over the mantle at one end of the
famous Peacock Room hangs *La Prin-
cesse du Pays de la Porcelaine*, Whistler's
deliberately oriental-like rendering of
Christine Spartali, an exotic beauty
who was the daughter of a Greek con-
sul general. It was not originally
painted for this room but the father
refused to pay for such a rendering of
his daughter, so Whistler retained the
work until Frederick R Leyland, the
British shipping magnate, bought it.
Leyland decided to give it a place of
honor in his London town house's
dining room, which he also intended
to hold his collection of Chinese porcelains. So it was that the young
Greek woman became 'The Princess
of the Land of Porcelain'; some of
Leyland's collection can also be seen
here. Designed by the British architect Thomas Jeckyll, the entire room
was eventually acquired by Charles
Freer, who installed it in his Detroit
home before it was moved intact to
the Freer Gallery.

Right

Girl with Lute, undated
Thomas Dewing
Oil on wood panel, 24 × 17¾ inches,
(61.4 × 45.4 cm)
(5.2)

This painting by the now largely forgotten American artist, Thomas Wilmer Dewing (1851-1938), is typical of
his many portraits of young women,
usually located in some timeless world
and rendered in a style that evokes
many other artists, from Vermeer to
Whistler to the French Impressionists.
In his day Dewing was immensely
popular, especially with rich collectors
of art, and Freer was by no means the
only benefactor of the Smithsonian
museums to bequeath their beloved
Dewings to the nation. Dewing was
born in Boston and trained in litho-
graphy and portrait drawing in Boston
and Albany, studied for a year (1880) in
Paris, then settled in New York City
where he stayed for the next 40 years.

Breakfast in the Loggia, 1910
John Singer Sargent
Oil on canvas, 20½ × 20½ inches,
(52.5 × 71.7 cm)
(17.182)

Breakfast in the Loggia portrays two friends, Eliza Wedgwood (in black) and Jane Emmet de Glehn, engaged in conversation as they sit in the morning light of an arcade in the Villa Torre Galli, near Florence, Italy. The play of sunlight and shadow, the interplay of colors, the variety of objects, all give Sargent the chance to display his bravura technique. Yet the effect is also like a short story by Sargent's friend, Henry James: one senses that these women are non-Italians and that the older woman has a story – and advice – for the younger one.

This was a world that Sargent knew intimately, as he had been born in Florence in 1856 to American parents and he lived most of his life in Europe, moving back and forth between there and Boston from 1887 onward. His fame as an artist came primarily from his upper-class American and English portraits. Sargent painted with flair and virtuosity, working quickly, and since his subjects usually felt flattered by his art, he found himself much in demand: he had completed 500 oil portraits by 1909. By 1910, when he did this watercolor, Sargent was determined to paint other subjects, moving on to landscape watercolors and ambitious murals.

Bust of a King, possibly Khosrow 1

Persia, Sassanian dynasty, mid sixth century AD
Silver, 12¹³⁄₁₆ × 9¼ inches
(32.8 × 23.7 cm)
(66.23)

As a result of his friendship with Whistler, Charles Freer came to appreciate the arts of Asia; among the vast collection of Asian works he left to the nation is this silver and gilt bust of a Persian king, an intriguing example of the metalwork of the Ancient Near East. Dating from the mid-sixth century, it is believed to depict Khosrow I (or Chosroe) (531-79 AD) of the Sassanid dynasty that ruled Persia (modern Iran) about 224-641 AD. Although regarded as a despotic and bloody ruler by those he conquered, he was considered just by his people and reformed the government, promoted education and rebuilt cities. The unusual crown that rests upon the domed head of the king is presumably symbolic of his power over the earth, as well as of the Zoroastrian religion he embraced. The arts of the Sassanian dynasty, drawing both on indigenous Persian traditions and the Greco-Roman world, are known for their high quality.

Left
Parvati
Chola dynasty, tenth century AD
Bronze, 36¼ inches high, (92.8 cm)
(29.84)

This elegant bronze statue of the
Hindu goddess Parvati was cast
during the Chola (or Colas) dynasty
that ruled southern India. Like most
Hindu deities, Parvati was believed to
have several names as well as several
aspects. She was the consort of the
deity Siva or Shiva, the god of destruction; as his wife, however, she
was also known as the goddess of
motherhood. She is usually represented as a mature and beautiful
woman, as here. The lugs on the ped-
estal were used when sculptures like
this were carried through the streets
during festival days.

Right
Bichitr Jahangir Preferring a Sufi Sheikh to Kings
Mughal miniature, c.1615–18
Color and gold on paper, 10 × 7⅛
inches (25.6 × 18.3 cm)
(42.15)

This miniature painting, actually a
page from an illuminated book,
depicts the Mughal Emperor Jahangir
offering a book to the white-bearded
sufi, a Moslem holy man, while
ignoring the three powerful kings, a
Turkish sultan, King James I of
England, and a Hindu potentate. The
Mughal dynasty was an Islamic
dynasty which conquered and ruled
most of India during the 1500s and
1600s. The Mughal Emperor not only
sits at a higher elevation, he is larger in
scale than the other figures, signifying
his earthly power; yet his enthrone-
ment on an hourglass signifies his
awareness that time on earth is but
fleeting, hence his preference for the
holy man.

Above

Blue and White Flask
Ming dynasty, early fifteenth
century
Porcelain, 18¾ × 16⁷⁄₁₆ × 8⅜ inches,
(48 × 42.2 × 21.5 cm)
(58.2)

The Ming Dynasty (1368-1644 AD)
was known for its many artistic
works. The prototypes for this elegant flask were actually utilitarian
metal canteens produced in Syria
during the thirteenth century.
Created by Chinese potters at the
Ching-te Chen kilns, the 19-inch
diameter flask is decorated mainly
with floral and leaf patterns that were
traditional in Chinese culture; however, the eight-pointed star at the
center refers to the Star of Islam,
further reflecting the origins of the design. Although Ming porcelains used
other pigments, they are especially
valued for this rich blue. The cobalt
pigment that produces the blue color-
ing in such objects was not used by
Chinese artists until they began to
obtain it from the Middle East in the
fourteenth century.

Right above

Lacquer pitcher

Momoyama period, early
sixteenth century
Red lacquer, 14 × 7⅝ inches,
(35.8 × 19.5 cm)
(58.2)

This Japanese lacquer pitcher was
made by priests of the Negoro temple
(in the province of Kii). As early as the
Kamakura period (fourteenth
century), these priests had begun to
devote themselves to making lacquer-
wares. Their original aim had been
simply to make the pitchers and other
containers needed for religious ceremonies or more ordinary purposes.
But, as the grace of this pitcher attests,
they developed the art of lacquerware
far beyond its utilitarian purposes. In
a few places the red lacquer has worn
away, revealing the black lacquer
undercoat; this sign of age makes such
a work even more valuable to those
who appreciate lacquerware.

Right below

Chinese jar with cover

Ming dynasty, fifteenth century
Gold studded with 21 semi-precious
stones, 3⅝ × 3¼ inches, (9.2 × 8.3 cm)
(52.29)

This small gold jar is believed to be
one of the eight gold pieces unearthed
from the tomb of Hsuan-te, Emperor
of China (1426-36) during the Ming
dynasty. However, the somewhat
crude setting of the jewels appears
more Tibetan than Chinese in style.
The gems include uncut sapphires and
rubies as well as pearls of irregular
shape; whoever made it, it is clearly
far too costly to have belonged to an
ordinary person. Clouds and winged
dragons are etched into the gold; the
mythical dragon was a symbol of
prosperity and fertility in ancient
China.

CHAPTER SIX

Hirshhorn Museum and Sculpture Garden

Financier Joseph H Hirshhorn once said that a visit to a museum was a little like a religious experience, in which evangelism, faith, humility and devotion ultimately lead to conversion. To this zealous devotee of art, the museum built to house his vast collection was probably something of a sanctuary. But most visitors see the Hirshhorn Museum and Sculpture Garden as a showcase of modern art – occasionally conventional but more often controversial.

Hirshhorn amassed his tremendous array of paintings and sculptures over a period of more than four decades. His first purchases were made in the 1930s, when he was a young businessman earning his fortune in the uranium market. Visits to New York museums and galleries, especially the Museum of Modern Art and the Whitney Museum, drew his interest away from traditional art and refocused it on newer forms. By the mid-1940s, Hirshhorn was known as New York's most dynamic collector of modern painting and sculpture; it was not unusual for him to hurry into a gallery, quickly purchase several paintings, and rush off again. He shied away from professional recommendations on value or aesthetic worth. Instead, Hirshhorn bought what appealed to him.

The collector's interests were never confined to a narrow time period, style or school. The works he acquired had been created over a period of nearly 200 years by American and European artists working in wildly divergent styles. Eventually, this great accumulation of art overflowed the bounds of two New York offices, a warehouse and his large estate in Greenwich, Connecticut.

By the early 1960s, the collection was internationally known. Offers came from several countries wanting to establish a museum for the collection, but when President Lyndon B Johnson proposed building a new museum specially for Hirshhorn's collection, the collector accepted. In 1966 Congress passed legislation creating the Hirshhorn Museum and Sculpture Garden. With the help of an additional donation of construction funds from Joseph Hirshhorn, the new building opened in 1974 with 4000 paintings, drawings and sculptures in its holdings.

Designed by architect Gordon Bunshaft, the unusual structure was designed to symbolize the unorthodox 'tradition' of the art it displayed. Cylindrical in shape and built of concrete, it is held up by four giant piers 14 feet high and is surrounded by a plaza. Seen from the outside, the solid circular walls are broken only by a narrow band of windows on one side but, stepping under the raised structure, the visitor discovers that the round building is really ring-shaped, with a fountain in the middle of the hollowed-out central courtyard. The inner 'walls' of the ring are glass windows, allowing in natural light. Sculptures line the inner circle, while outer galleries hold paintings. The plaza around the building and the adjacent landscaped Sculpture Garden hold the more monumental pieces.

The collection is remarkable for its breadth and scope. Visitors can follow the development of modern Western sculpture, beginning with traditional late-eighteenth-century busts and figures and culminating in the infinitely diverse works of contemporary times. It includes such nineteenth-century precursors of modernism as Honoré Daumier's bronze satiric caricatures, Rodin's powerful, larger-than-life figures, and Edgar Degas' small bronze ballerinas. The true beginnings of modern sculpture can be seen in the stylized heads of Constantin Brancusi: features are all but lost, blending together in a smooth, graceful form.

A great explosion of creativity follows, with sculptures that can be classified broadly as Cubist, Abstract, Surreal, Op, Pop and Constructivist – although many are difficult to pigeonhole. Visitors to the Hirshhorn may alternately feel moved, intrigued, and sometimes baffled, by works which show the endless possibilities of the medium. Included are Henry Moore's serene, rounded figures, the Cubist bronzes of Pablo Picasso, Jean Arp's fantasy forms, Alexander Calder's mobiles and stabiles, Joseph Cornell's intriguing boxes, Louise Nevelson's large totem-like wooden pieces and David Smith's steel constructions.

The paintings at the Hirshhorn focus mainly on American art, although significant European artists are represented through major works. Here again, creative innovation seems to have no limits. The late nineteenth- and early twentieth-century American selection includes a large group of more traditional works such as Thomas Eakins' psychologically penetrating portraits, and paintings by impressionists Mary Cassatt, Childe Hassam, John Singer Sargent and William Merritt Chase. Among early modernist

Above A striking contrast to the Victorian brick architecture of the original Smithsonian buildings, the sleek, modern Hirshhorn Museum opened in 1974.

works are the paintings of Maurice Prendergast, Robert Henri, Arthur B Davies and other members of 'The Eight', also known as 'The Ashcan School' by critics who found their radical depictions of urban life unappealing. Arthur Dove, Marsden Hartley and Georgia O'Keeffe are among the collection's representatives of the Photo-Secession group.

The Hirshhorn is strong in its presentation of Abstract Expressionist paintings. The movement can be traced through the works of artists including Willem de Kooning, Robert Motherwell, Kenneth

Noland, Jackson Pollock, Mark Rothko, Jasper Johns, Larry Rivers and Frank Stella. The new literalism that arose in antithesis to abstract art is represented by painters as diverse as Robert Rauschenberg, Red Grooms and Richard Estes. The smaller group of twentieth-century European paintings contains important works by Fernand Léger, Balthus, Joan Miró, Piet Mondrian and René Magritte.

The collection has tripled in size since Joseph Hirshhorn made his original gift to the public, growing along with recent movements, themes and styles in modern art. As much twentieth-century art continues to be wildly innovative and experimental, the only ongoing tradition here may be the one begun by its founder: always seek out and welcome something new and different.

Left
The Burghers of Calais, 1885-95
Auguste Rodin
Bronze

Auguste Rodin (1840-1917) is one of the most significant figures in the history of Western sculpture. *The Burghers of Calais*, which dominates the Hirshhorn's sunken sculpture garden, was commissioned in 1884 by the town of Calais in France. The larger-than-life figures speak of the suffering of the townsmen who were given as hostages to King Edward III of England in exchange for lifting the siege of Calais during the Hundred Years War. The town surrendered in 1377. Dressed in sackcloth, with nooses around their necks, the burghers await their execution. Some critics have suggested that the three stages of life can be read through their demeanor: the strength and rebellion of youth, the quiet respectability of middle age and the weariness of the elderly.

Above
Mrs Thomas Eakins, c.1899
Thomas Eakins
Oil on canvas, 20⅛ × 16⅛ inches
(51 × 40.8 cm)
Gift of Joseph H Hirshhorn, 1966
(66.1522)

The 'father' of modern American portrait painting and, many think, still the country's greatest portrait painter, Thomas Eakins (1844-1916) is known for his realistic paintings. Not surprisingly, Eakins was a keen student of human anatomy; his famous works *The Gross Clinic* and *The Agnew Clinic* reveal this interest. Eakins also worked in the medium of photography as well as oil, often using family and friends as models for his studies and sometimes working from photographs. He created likenesses that were psychologically penetrating rather than flattering. Feminine 'charm' was almost always missing from Eakins' portraits of women, which often showed the sitter's anxiety and introspection. Eakins believed that ideal beauty could never compare to reality, and he tried to 'peer deeper into the heart of American life.' In *Mrs Thomas Eakins* all the lines of age and experience, reflecting the struggles of life, appear in this strikingly realistic painting of the artist's wife.

Sleeping Muse 1, 1909–11
Constantin Brancusi
Marble, 7 × 10⅝ × 8 inches
(17.8 × 26.8 × 20.3 cm)
Gift of Joseph H Hirshhorn, 1966
(66.610)

Constantin Brancusi (1876–1957) was born in Romania but studied and worked in Paris under the prominent French sculptor Marius Jean Antonin Mercie, after turning down Rodin's offer to work in his studio. Brancusi's radical, spare style was a considerable contrast to that of both Mercie and Rodin and made the controversial Romanian a forerunner of the Modernist movement.

Brancusi's *Sleeping Muse I* is sculpted of white marble; although the head suggests pure form, seemingly owing nothing to any individual head, critics have suggested that Brancusi in fact modelled his muse on his friend Baroness Renée Franchon. The *Sleeping Muse*, like its name, seems almost classical in its essence, although individual features are subsumed to the abstract form. Eyes, brows, nose and mouth all blend together as part of a single whole. The *Sleeping Muse* is nonetheless more representational than the same artist's *Prometheus*, also in the Hirshhorn, whose features disappear altogether into a sleek void.

Beach at Gloucester, c.1912–14
Maurice Brazil Prendergast
Oil on canvas, 30⅝ × 43⅛ inches
(77.9 × 109.3 cm)
Gift of the Joseph H Hirshhorn
Foundation, 1966 (66.4130)

Maurice Prendergast (1859–1924) exhibited with The Eight, a group of
American Modernist painters including Arthur B Davies, John Sloan and
Robert Henri which opposed the
established world of art and rejected
academicism. While The Eight was
ridiculed by some critics as the 'Ashcan School' because many of the
artists portrayed the realities of common life, Prendergast himself was
better known for his fascination with
color, and was more influenced by the
Post-Impressionists than by the Real-
ists. Resembling mosaics, his canvases were often naïve and simple,
covered by quick, free brushstrokes.
In his 60s, Prendergast often altered,
or virtually repainted, many of his
earlier works. In consequence many
paintings of this period have thick
surfaces, with barely perceptible
forms from earlier paintings showing
through.

The Beach at Gloucester may cover
nearly all of a 'lost' painting (preserved only by a photograph), *The
Beach,* which it resembles. Like many
of Prendergast's oils and watercolors,
The Beach at Gloucester shows a plea-
sant, almost idyllic, scene.

Left
Painting No. 47, Berlin, 1914–15
Marsden Hartley
Oil on canvas, 33½ × 31⅝ inches
(100.1 × 81.3 cm)
Gift of Joseph H Hirshhorn, 1972
(72.148)

Marsden Hartley's *Painting Number 47* commemorates the artist's romance with a young German officer, Lieutenant Karl von Freyburg, who was killed when World War I broke out. The painting includes an abstract series of German war motifs containing flags and symbols such as the Iron Cross. The initials 'K.v.F.' in the painting are those of Lieutenant von Freyburg.

Above
People of Chilmark, 1920
Thomas Hart Benton
Oil on canvas, 65⅝ × 77⅝ inches
(166.5 × 197.3 cm)
Gift of the Joseph H Hirshhorn
Foundation, 1966 (66.468)

Thomas Hart Benton (1890–1975) is often credited with founding the school of painting known as The American Scene. As its name suggests, the emphasis was on distinctively American themes and topics. Using his own form of Expressionism, Benton concentrated on painting American themes in a graphic, dramatic style, often in mural form portraying scenes from the American past.

In his *People of Chilmark*, the stances of the workers, mariners and athletes suggest those of classic Olympian heroes, yet these are distinctively American figures. Benton's Depression-era murals depicting modern industrialization reflect the artist's ambivalence about the growth and progress of the urban United States. After 1935, Benton left New York and concentrated on regional scenes, often turning to documented episodes from the past and portraying the early pioneers and explorers.

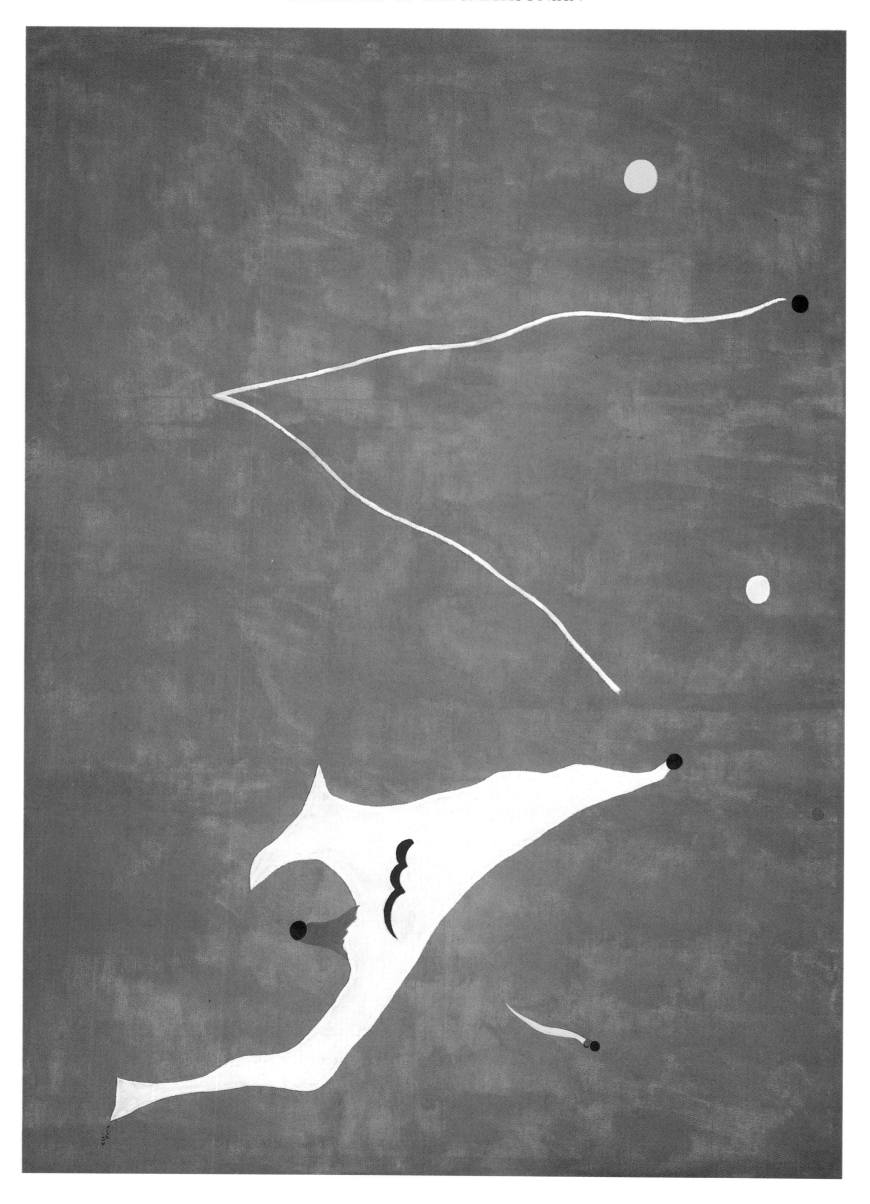

Left
Circus Horse, 1927
Joan Miró
Oil and pencil on burlap, 76¾ × 110⅜
inches (195 × 280.2 cm)
Gift of the Joseph H Hirshhorn
Foundation, 1972 (72.202)

Surrealists have found much to in-
spire them in circuses – movement,
play, fantasy and danger. In 1927 both
Spanish artist Joan Miro and
American sculptor/painter Alexander
Calder worked on groups of circus
paintings. Miro once said of his work:
'For me, a form is never something
abstract. It is always a man, a bird or
something else. For me a painting is
never form for form's sake,' In Miro's
Circus Horse, the abstract shapes suggest the subject matter: one senses the
motion of a leaping horse in Miro's
abstract fantasy.

Above
Maude Stettiner, 1931
Pavel Tchelitchew
Oil on canvas, 51⅛ × 35 inches
(130.9 × 89.6 cm)
Gift of the Joseph H Hirshhorn
Foundation, 1966 (66.4889)

Russian-born Pavel Tchelitchew
spent years in Europe before emig-
rating to the United States in 1938.
During the 1920s Tchelitchew devised
a method of multiple imagery and
varied perspectives in his works,
creating fantasy-like settings that
linked him to the Surrealist movement. He also painted many portraits,
often in a more traditional style, and
was admired by Gertrude Stein and
Dame Edith Sitwell, both of whom
sat for him. Here the subject is an art
lover who worked in a gallery and
later owned a bookshop dealing in art
books. Tchelitchew probably met
Maude through her brother Jacques
Stettiner, a painter. Although the
painting takes the name of its subject,
it could easily be called *Study in Red*.

Left
Delusions of Grandeur, 1948
René-François-Ghislain Magritte
Oil on canvas, 39⅛ × 32⅛ inches
(99.2 × 81.5 cm)
Gift of the Joseph H Hirshhorn
Foundation, 1966 (66.3199)

René Magritte is known for his un-
nerving juxtaposition of everyday
scenes with fantasies of the absurd.
Clear yet dream-like, his paintings
surprise the observer, often with an
eerie wittiness. In *Delusions of
Grandeur*, the headless, torso is
divided into three sections of dimin-
ishing size. The softness of the white
clouds is broken by rectangular sky-
blue blocks. Calmly and incon-
gruously, a hot air balloon quietly
rises above the still seascape, as an un-
flickering candle stands burning in
bright daylight. The Belgian Surrealist painter seemed intrigued by the
image of the three-part torso. He re-
peated it in larger paintings and super-
vised the casting of a bronze sectioned
torso in 1967.

Above
Covenant, 1949
Barnett Newman
Oil on canvas, 47¾ × 59⅝ inches
(121.3 × 151.4 cm)
Gift of the Joseph H Hirshhorn
Foundation, 1972 (72.2123)

Along with his contempories Clyf-
ford Still and Mark Rothko, Barnett
Newman (1905-1970) has been called a
color-field painter. Newman often, as
here, divided broad areas of a single
color by narrow vertical lines at
various intervals. Critics praised

Newman's use of color, yet the artist
himself felt that his strength lay in his
composition. *Covenant* was painted
during an especially productive time:
between October 1948 and the end of
1949, Newman finished twenty canvases, many with biblical titles. Later
paintings such as *Who's Afraid of Red,
Yellow & Blue IV?* made use of
primary color blocks. Some critics
have seen Newman as a precursor of
the minimalist art of the 1960s, in
which color-field painting played an
important part, and he was an important influence on younger artists.

Left
Woman with Baby Carriage,
1950
Pablo Picasso
Bronze, 80⅛ × 57 × 24 inches
(293.2 × 144.7 × 60.9 cm)
Gift of the Joseph H Hirshhorn
Foundation, 1972 (72.233)

If one person can be said to have
dominated twentieth-century art,
surely that artist was Pablo Picasso,
who was born in Spain in 1881.
Picasso worked in almost every
medium; painting, sculpture, ceramics, textiles – there seemed to be no
limits to his creativity. In fact, his
mere signature scrawled on a napkin
fetched a high price at an art auction!
Woman with Baby Carriage (1950) is an
almost life-sized bronze made out of
found objects which Picasso picked
up on walks near his studio.

Above
Rapt at Rappaport's, 1952
Stuart Davis
Oil on canvas, 52 × 40 inches
(131.8 × 101.4 cm)
Gift of the Joseph H Hirshhorn
Foundation, 1966 (66.1165)

American artist Stuart Davis (1894–
1964) was one of the most influential
painters of the first half of this
century. He favored two-dimension-
ality in his paintings, as in *Rapt at Rappaport's* shown here. Davis once said:
'I always start with something I have
just seen, remembered music, or
something that is immediately in
front of me, or something I read. That
is part of the subject matter, as is the
mood I am in. Whether good or bad, I
regard the mood I am in as part of the
subject.' Davis appears to have been
in a positive mood much of the time,
as his work is generally up-beat and
jazzy. His frequently poster-like
paintings often contain words and
bright colors. Sometimes letters seem
to dance, and words play, pun-like, as
in the title here. In 1991-1992, Davis
was honored with a major retrospec-
tive exhibition at New York's Metro-
politan Museum of Art.

Above
Point of Tranquillity, 1959–60
Morris Louis
Magna on canvas, 101¾ × 135¾ inches
(258.2 × 344.9 cm)
Gift of the Joseph H Hirshhorn
Foundation, 1966 (66.3111)

Something of a loner in the art world, Baltimore painter Morris Louis (1912–1962) rarely discussed his work. One of the so-called 'color-field' painters, Louis produced misty, abstract effects through staining techniques. By leaving out an undercoat and pouring thinned acrylic paint directly on to large canvases, Louis created transparent fields of color. The effect was expansive and flowing; sometimes, as here, vivid colors overlapped. At other times, the artist experimented with muted effects. *Point of Tranquillity* belonged to a series known as 'Florals'.

Right
Two Discs, 1965
Alexander Calder
Painted steel plate and bolts, 306 × 328 × 208 inches (777.3 × 833.2 × 528.3 cm)
Gift of the Joseph H Hirshhorn
Foundation, 1966 (66.791)

Humor may be the most important unifying ingredient in the vast array of works completed by the twentieth century American artist Alexander Calder. Whether in his early wooden toys, line drawings of the circus, abstract paintings, playful mobiles, or jet planes painted for Braniff airlines, Calder's work can bring a smile to the face of the most serious art-lover. While this painted steel stabile is 25 feet tall, many of Calder's stabiles grew gargantuan in size, requiring iron works factories to execute them and cranes to help piece them together. Soaring and arching, Calder's stabiles have been place in cities around the world. A four-part tunnel was placed over a crossroad in Spoleto, Italy, in 1962, and a 70-foot stabile went up in Montreal in 1967.

Diner, 1971
Richard Estes
Oil on canvas, 40⅛ × 50 inches
(101.8 × 126.8 cm)
Museum Purchase 1977 (77.75)

Following decades of emphasis on Abstract Expressionism in the art world, photo-realism – virtually its artistic opposite – became a major force during the 1970s. An overnight sensation among the photo-realists was Richard Estes, whose cityscapes could easily be taken for photographs. A resident of New York City, Estes painted what he saw: streets, high-rise buildings and cars. After the 1960s, Estes seldom included people in his paintings, preferring to concentrate on the urban scene itself. In *Diner*, meticulous attention is paid to the light and shadows upon the chrome of the telephone booths and the diner itself. Nothing is left out: the sidewalk and brownstone slabs have their share of cracks and blemishes, phonebooks are in their holders, and dials may be seen on the rotary phones. Estes' paintings lack the psychological subtlety and insight of another realist of urban America, Edward Hopper, but nonetheless make a clear artistic statement.

Above
**Elegy to the Spanish Republic
129**, 1974
Robert Burns Motherwell
Acrylic and charcoal on canvas,
96 × 120 inches (245.8 × 307.2 cm)
Museum Purchase 1981 (81.248)

Between 1949-1976, American artist
Robert Motherwell completed 150
paintings inspired by the horrors of
the Spanish Civil War. The series uses
few colors, concentrating on black
and white. These colors, Motherwell
once said, 'tend to be the protago-
nists.' Of this series of Elegies
Motherwell has commented, 'The
Elegies use a basic pictorial language,
in which I seem to have hit on an
"archetypal" image. Even people
who are actively hostile to abstract art
are, on occasion, moved by it, but do
not know why.'

Right
The Square in June, 1983
Avigdor Arikha
Oil on linen, 76⅞ × 51¼ inches
(195.1 × 130 cm)
Museum Purchase 1983 (83.152)

This oil painting by the Israeli artist
Avigdor Arikha, painted in Paris,
captures the light and shadows of a
particular time and day (June 9, 1983,
to be precise) as they play across the
corner buildings of a square, thus
turning this normal, natural scene
into something almost formal and
abstract. Arikha was born in Buko-
vina, Romania, in 1929, and emigrated to Palestine in 1944; he studied
in Jerusalem (1946-49) and at the Ecole
des Beaux Arts in Paris (1949-51) and
has since exhibited in Israel, Europe
and the USA. He has done drawings
and prints but is best known for his
oils, which often convey his concern
for the abstract and formal elements
of painting, reflecting perhaps his
studies under the major Israeli artist,
Mordechai Ardon.

CHAPTER SEVEN

National Museum of Natural History

The National Museum for Natural History features the grandest and oldest, biggest and most valuable wonders of nature. In the central rotunda, the world's largest African bush elephant towers above visitors, his trunk poised high in the air. This giant specimen stands 14 feet tall at the shoulder and weighs in at no less than eight tons. Children point and stare at the 90-foot-long skeleton of Diplodocus, one of the longest creatures ever to walk upon the earth. Crowds share tales of destruction and death, recalling the 'curse' of the fabled 45.5-carat Hope Diamond, the largest and most famous blue diamond in the world.

Visitors see a dazzling showcase, with prizes collected from the depths of the sea and chiseled from the earth's crust. The riches here have fallen from the skies and been gathered in remotest lands – and also on the moon – or have been created by the skill and ingenuity of early civilizations.

But what happens at the National Museum of Natural History goes on mostly behind the scenes. This monumental structure actually reveals little of itself to the five million people who crowd its exhibits every year. The 100-million-cubic-foot Museum of Natural History has almost 20 acres of floor space, and yet it only shows about one fifth of its area to the public. There is an unseen labyrinth with no fewer than 1200 separate hidden rooms, attics, hallways, chambers and basements, serving as libraries and laboratories, storage areas and x-ray chambers, darkrooms and study halls, rooms where autopsies are done, sculpture and painting studios, computer data-processing centers – and rooms and more rooms for research.

Here researchers catalogue, examine, conserve and occasionally dissect the 63 million specimens of minerals, animals and vegetables and the artifacts of early and primitive man that fill this hidden maze. Hallways are stacked from floor to ceiling with human skeletons in boxes; attics are lined with large mammals, appearing to stand peacefully in silent rows. Thousands of animal pelts hang from hooks, while eggshells as big as footballs and as small as buttons, black, yellow, blue and mottled, fill hundreds and hundreds of drawers. Reptiles and fish are preserved in multi-sized bottles of formaldehyde, and 26 million bugs stay pinned in tiny containers, their vital statistics recorded in giant data-

banks. Odd artifacts are also tucked away, including the hide of General Pershing's horse, shrunken heads and a dragon in a freezer.

The museum's seven departments – Anthropology, Botany, Entomology, Invertebrate Zoology, Mineral Sciences, Paleobiology and Vertebrate Zoology – all work toward the unified goal of understanding what the natural world is really about. The seemingly infinite number of natural specimens and man-made artifacts here are safely stored and preserved for the gradual edification of humankind. At the National Museum of Natural History, they say that one just never knows what may some day be of use.

Early collections of natural objects and primitive artifacts were known as 'cabinets of curiosities.' Over hundreds of years, as collections have continued to grow, wonder about our world has evolved into study and understanding. The National Museum of Natural History is devoted to knowledge and science; it was not founded as such but gradually evolved. After the Smithsonian's first Secretary, scientist Joseph Henry, moved into the Castle-on-the-Mall in 1849, he hired Spencer Fullerton Baird as his assistant. Baird was a collector, and brought along with him a few thousand items of interest, which he gave as a gift to the Smithsonian: stuffed birds and mammals, skeletons and jars of reptiles and fishes. This early collection of natural objects increased in 1858 when the Smithsonian received from a quasi-official organization, the National Institution for the Promotion of Science and Useful Arts, another group of thousands of man-made artifacts and natural specimens.

In 1878, Baird succeeded Henry as Secretary of the Smithsonian. Under his direction the Arts and Industries Building, originally called the National Museum, was built. This was designed to show off exhibits from the 1876 Philadelphia Centennial Exposition, but eventually many of the Smithsonian's natural objects went there. Donations from science-minded individuals and groups kept pouring in, however, and much more space still was needed. When Baird died in

Right The National Museum of Natural History, built in 1911, showcases millions of displays from tiny beetles to enormous dinosaurs in some eleven acres of floor space.

1897, the Smithsonian had in its holdings over two and a half million specimens, with many more to come.

The turn of the century was a period of intense scientific and naturalist interest in the United States. This was the era of President Teddy Roosevelt, hunter, naturalist, conservationist. In 1909, after completing his second term in office, Roosevelt led a Smithsonian-sponsored safari in Africa and returned with a gift of 12000 new specimens. By the time the Natural History building was erected in 1911 under Secretary Charles Walcott's administration, the Smithsonian was gaining about 250,000 new items each year.

The new building was meant to be monumental both in size and stature. Its Corinthian portico faced the Mall, and a 125-foot-tall rotunda (praised by architects but opposed by practical curators) graced its center. Eleven acres of floor space allowed room, finally, for everything: enough room, in fact, for the Smithsonian's National Collection of Fine Arts to move in temporarily and be displayed in its own gallery space. And yet the gifts kept coming by the thousands and hundreds of thousands. In the 1960s, with new objects and specimens coming in at the rate of one million each year, two new seven-story wings were erected. The great museum doubled in size, giving it the vast space it has today.

Its character has changed over time. Gone are the old mahogany and glass display cases that held all those beetles and bones. Despite the great age of many of its specimens (the oldest rock ever found – 3.8 billion years – has a place in these halls) the museum seems to have grown younger with the years. No longer just for scientists, although a few hundred of them are working there, the museum draws millions of children and adults each year. And no wonder. A world's worth of amazing things can be seen and experienced here, along with a number of extra-terrestrial items.

In the Dinosaur Hall, a life-size model of a Pteranodon with its 40-foot wingspan glides overhead, above the horned Triceratops, a 'recent' dinosaur which died out only 65 million years ago. Huge Diplodocus, with his graceful elongated neck, dominates the room. His bones were shipped here in 1923 in 36 large crates; a gigantic puzzle that took 35 man years to reassemble.

Representing the Ice Age which ended 10000 years ago are the fossils of huge beasts that lived at the time of early man: the slow-moving, 20-foot-tall giant ground sloth; the woolly mammoth with his great curling tusks. Nearby a beautifully carved single tusk, almost 25000 years old, shows off the talents of some skilled native artisan.

The Sea Life Hall, darkly blue-green, mimics the depths of the ocean. Swimming through the air is a life-sized model of the largest animal that has ever lived; arching his great back, the Blue Whale overhead is 92 feet long and represents a species that sometimes grows to 300,000 pounds. Myriad specimens of the deep are here: mollusks, crustaceans, fish, sponges. Two real aquariums containing 500 live species simulate the natural conditions on the coast of Maine and the coral reefs of the Caribbean.

The Rock and Mineral Hall contains a treasury of great chunks of gold, gleaming opals and brilliant crystal 'gardens'. Shaped by many factors, some of the crystals resemble flowers, sea creatures or man-made monuments, created in an array of opulent colors. Less appealing to the eye, but even rarer, are the large iron meteorites that traveled through space before crash-landing on our planet, and the rocks brought back from the surface of the moon.

When cut and polished by skilled artists, precious natural stones turn into dazzling gems. In the museum's famed Hall of Gems, over 1000 rare jewels of incalculable worth are on display. The legendary Hope Diamond carries a mystique all its own. Other historic jewels include the 300-year old sapphire and diamond Spanish Inquisition necklace, the 127-carat Portuguese Diamond, and the 330-carat sapphire, the Star of India.

Here too the animals of land and sky can be found: skeletons that come in endless sizes and shapes, vertebrates and invertebrates, frogs and snakes, stuffed species from every continent and live insects that hop and chirp in an Insect Zoo. But human beings are part of nature, and the Museum shows off the ingenuity, creativity and diversity of our own species. It exhibits a huge multitude of artifacts from ancient, primitive and developing cultures, including a great stone figure from Easter Island, ornate Asian musical instruments, pre-Columbian sculptures, African masks, Roman glassware, Native American totem poles and Egyptian mummies.

An art museum, a science museum, the world's most fabulous jewelry store, a giant warehouse for collections and a world-class research facility, The National Museum of Natural History is all these things and more: a place of fascination, beauty and wonder in which to satisfy curiosity.

Left Assembling the huge skeletons of dinosaurs and other prehistoric creatures for display at the National Museum of Natural History has always required delicate teamwork.

Above
Dinosaur Hall

Diplodocus longus, one of the longest creatures ever to set foot on the earth, is the great centerpiece of the paleontology exhibits in Dinosaur Hall. The 90-foot, 11-ton, herbivorous reptile, which may have been an amphibious swamp-dweller, lived 145 million years ago in the Late Jurassic age. This towering specimen was chiseled out of the sandstone that surrounded it in Utah in 1923. The equivalent of 35 man years of effort was spent in its reassembly. A 50-foot long steel support holds the fossil's spine in place. Other exhibits in Dinosaur Hall include a soaring model of a pterosaur with a 40-foot wingspan.

Right
Giant Ground Sloth

Originating in South America, the Giant Ground Sloths came into North America during what scientists call the 'Great American Faunal Interchange', when animals crossed the newly formed Isthmus of Panama from South America into North America. Distant and long extinct cousins of the modern sloth, these great mammals were literally elephantine in size. The 20-foot tall beast weighed several tons and had claws and toes that curled inward, making it clumsy and slow-going. Like the elephant, the sloth was a vegetarian that fed on twigs and leaves of trees.

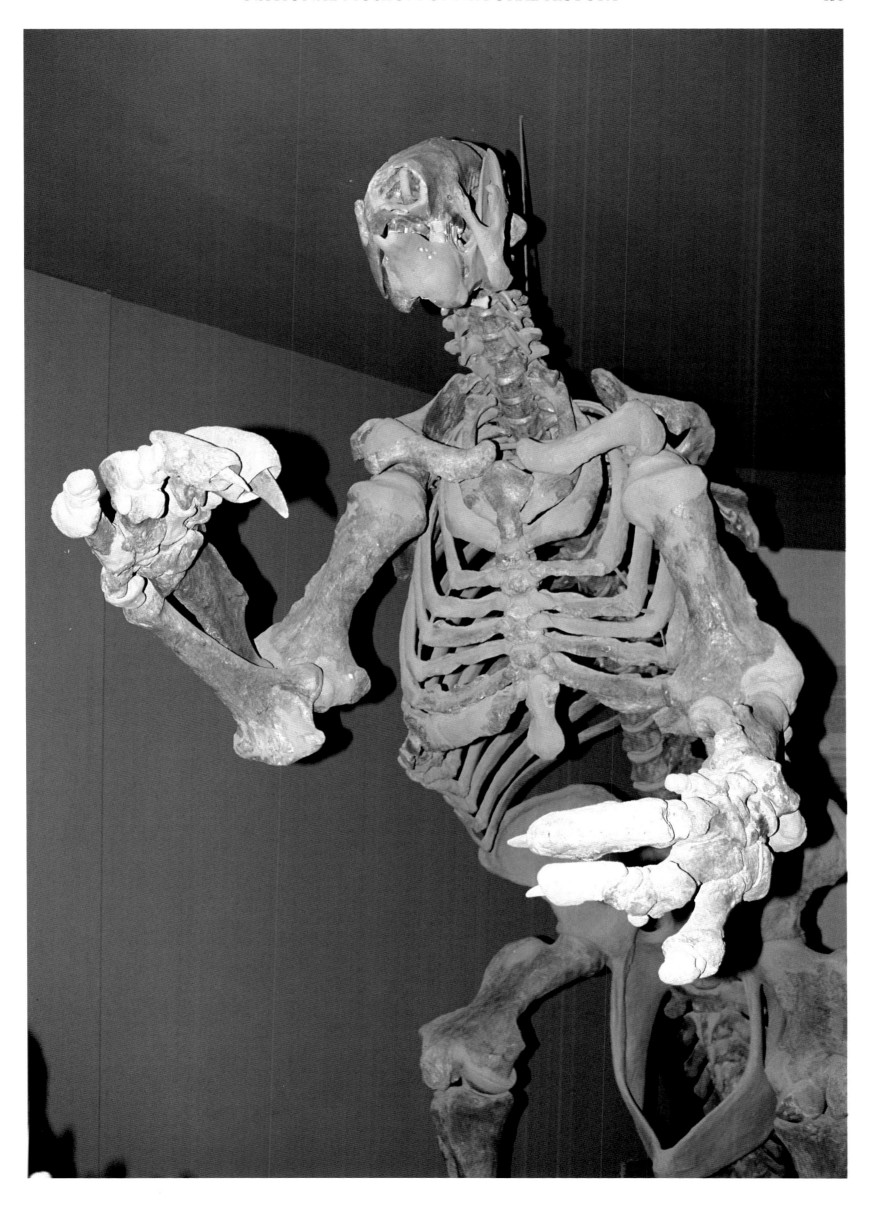

Above
Ring Meteorite, Tucson, Arizona

The museum's collection includes a number of meteorites, cosmic objects that fall to earth. This is one of the most unusual, not just because of its shape but because its high silicon content suggests that it was formed in an environment with exceptionally little oxygen. Weighing 1,371 pounds and measuring three by four feet, the meteorite was found near Tucson, Arizona. While its journey to the Smithsonian cannot rival its voyage through space, it was lengthy by earth standards: overland from Arizona to California in 1863, then by boat to the Isthmus of Panama, overland again to the Atlantic Ocean, and north by boat to Washington DC.

Right above
Seeds of Change Exhibition

The globe was irrevocably and monumentally changed by Columbus' 1492 voyage, which landed him in the West Indies. But is his journey something to celebrate or to mourn? This question is tackled in the Smithsonian's largest exhibition ever mounted, 'Seeds of Change', which opened in 1991. The seeds exchanged between the Old World and the New World – sugar, corn, disease, the horse and the potato – altered societies, fed some populations while they decimated others, but undeniably brought changes in both hemispheres that shaped our modern world.

Right below
Wulfenite, Mexico

This yellow crystal of wulfenite with mimetite, found in Mexico, is one of many gorgeous minerals in the museum. Crystals form a geometric pattern determined by their molecular structure; the shape is never random. An exquisite pattern may result as a scaffolding effect is created following the atomic structure. Like most crystals, wulfenite is made of a combination of various elements, in this case, lead, molybdenum and oxygen.

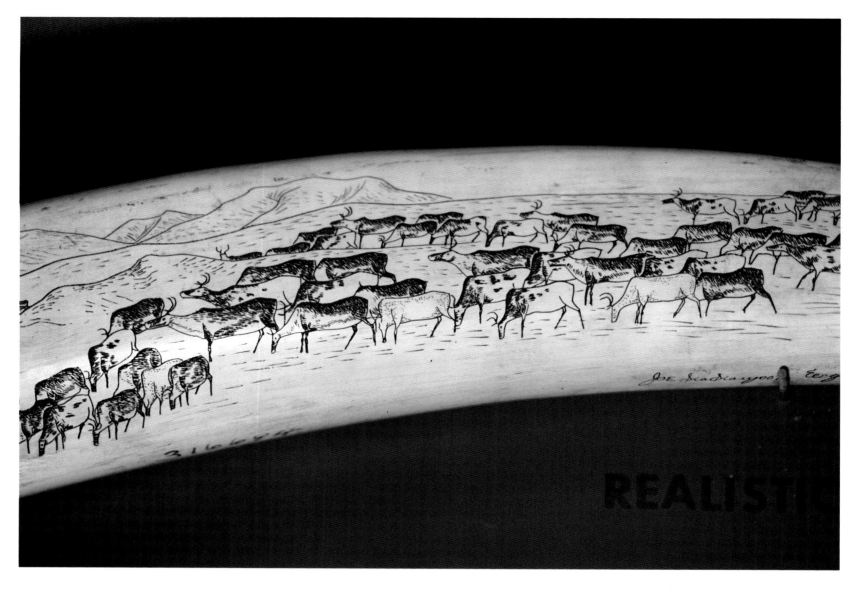

Walrus Tusk carved by Bering Sea Eskimos

One of the most impressive galleries in the National Museum of Natural History is devoted to the Native Peoples of the Americas. The geographical range .alone is enormous: there are exhibits showing life as far north as Port Barrow in the Arctic and as far south as Tierra del Fuego and Cape Horn in South America. This handsome walrus tusk carving was made by Eskimos who live by the Bering Sea between Siberia and Alaska.

For generations, the Bering Sea Eskimos have hunted the walrus and used its skin for clothing and its flesh for food. In addition, skillful artists carved walrus tusks into ornate sculptures or etched them with designs showing life in the far north. Many of the finest items in the museum's Eskimo collection are in the Nelson Collection started by Edward R Nelson, an army officer who explored the Bering Sea coasts in the 1880s. Today these carvings are highly sought after collectors' items, prized by all who admire Native American art.

Above
Hope Diamond

The 45.52 carat Hope Diamond takes its name from Henry Philip Hope, an English collector whose family owned the diamond for several generations. This enormous diamond, the largest blue diamond in the world, has a romantic and somewhat ill-starred history, which may have been invented by French jeweler Pierre Cartier in order to attract a wealthy Amercian buyer. As the story goes, the diamond was stolen out of the eye of an Indian idol by a greedy merchant and sold to King Louis XIV. The merchant was killed by wild dogs, while Louis XIV, known as 'the Sun King', died a hated figure. Within a generation, the inheritors of the Hope, Marie Antoinette and Louis XVI, were guillotined, while later owners variously committed suicide, went insane, were shot and stabbed. Whatever the truth of these rumors, the fact remains that Cartier's American buyer, heiress Evelyn Walsh McLean, wore the necklace frequently for more than 40 years, without incident. Mrs McLean sold the great blue diamond to New York jeweler Harry Winston, who donated it to the Smithsonian in 1958.

Following pages
African Bush Elephant

This great African Bush Elephant from Angola stands in the center of the Museum's great rotunda. At its death, the elephant was approximately 50 years old and weighed 8 tons.

Above
Easter Island Figure

Easter Island lies some 2000 miles west of Chile, to which it belongs. Its inhabitants speak a Polynesian language and are perhaps best known for creating the remarkable monolithic stone figures that many have taken to be idols. Some of the idols are simply enormous heads, while others, like this one standing 10 feet tall, include a torso. Little is known about the figures: do they, in fact, show deities? Or the spirits of ancestors? Are they of great antiquity, or were they made as recently as the seventeenth century AD? What is known is that the idols are carved out of tufa, a soft volcanic stone, and that they range from 10 to 40 feet in height, weighing as much as 50 tons.

Above right
Samurai Armor

Over the years, many gifts have been given to US presidents by world leaders in the name of diplomacy and friendship. Some, showing the splendid craftsmanship of artisans of foreign cultures, are now in the collections of the Smithsonian. The Emperor of Japan gave this suit of Samurai armor to President Theodore Roosevelt in 1905, when the Treaty of Portsmouth ending the Russo-Japanese War was signed. The ferocious mask was executed in the nineteenth century, while the ornate helmet bowl was made in the early sixteenth century. The samurai were the knights of feudal Japan, who dominated society from the twelfth through the nineteenth centuries, when they were outlawed; they are still revered in Japan today.

Above
Egyptian Mummy Coffin of Tenet-Khonsu, c.1000 BC

Mummification was first practiced in ancient Egypt more than 5000 years ago. The embalmed, wrapped bodies of the dead, known as mummies, were sometimes encased in more than one coffin. This is what happened to Tenet-Khonsu, a high priestess of the god Amon-Ra, from the 21st dynasty, c.1000 BC, who was buried inside a double coffin (only the outer coffin is shown here). Most coffins bear designs illustrating Egyptian mythology, meant to protect the deceased. The ancient Egyptians believed that the soul might re-enter the body after death, and often buried treasures and embalmed food offerings with the deceased. It was not just people who were embalmed: many mummies of cats, considered a sacred animal, have been found in Egpyt.

Above right
Carved Wooden Feline Figure

This six-inch tall, carved wooden figure of a member of the cat family was made six or seven centuries ago by the little-known native American inhabitants of Key Marco, Florida. the piece is especially rare because wooden objects are usually destroyed by the effects of hot, tropical climates, whereas hot, dry climates – such as Egpyt's – preserve objects beautifully. While this feline figure seems similar to some Egyptian or Meso-American carvings, no connection with these cultures has been established. We cannot say whether this figure represented a sacred animal or was simply a sculpture portraying a local creature. Still, most viewers are struck by the figure's power and mystery: with the head of a cat, the haunches of a woman and the musculature of a male athlete, this small figure reminds us that art is not the exclusive preserve of named and recognized artists.

CHAPTER EIGHT

National Portrait Gallery

Although Congress made an early step toward creating a portrait collection in 1857 by commissioning a group of portraits of American presidents, it did not establish the National Portrait Gallery until 1962. The museum opened in 1968, together with the National Museum of American Art, in the historical Old Patent Office Building. The monumental Greek Revival building was once a showcase for the patent models of America's inventors. Now just a few of these remain for nostalgia's sake, filling a vintage display case by the museum's architectural gem, the Great Hall.

These days, portraits of Abraham Lincoln and Civil War era heroes cover the walls of the Great Hall. Yet even if the walls were bare, this gallery would not seem lacking in artistic treasures. With its elaborately tiled floor, ornate marble and gilt pilasters and columns, balustrades and a kaleidoscopic stained-glass dome atop a rotunda, the Great Hall is a dazzling example of Victorian Renaissance style. Bas-relief Greco-Roman-style cameos of great American inventors – Fulton, Franklin, Whitney and Jefferson – grace the rotunda walls.

Other parts of the National Portrait Gallery are elegant but less distracting, allowing visitors to focus on the subjects at hand: the 4500 portraits of significant Americans. In a sense, the museum serves as a memorial: with the exception of presidents of the United States, portraits are not accepted for the permanent collection or public display until 10 years after the subject's death. Only under special circumstances are portraits of living Americans accepted for later addition.

The Gallery is as much a museum of art as of history. Among the hundreds of artists represented, some of them little known or unidentified, are many luminaries of American painting: John Singleton Copley, Charles Wilson Peale, Mary Cassatt, John Singer Sargent, Thomas Hart Benton, and that popular folksy illustrator, Norman Rockwell. Photographers include Mathew Brady, Edward Weston, Edward Steichen, Man Ray and Walker Evans. And the wide range of portrait sculptures includes busts by Jo Davidson and Paul Manship along with Marisol's wooden caricatures.

Who are their subjects, and what have they done to earn entrée into this exclusive club? A Hall of Presidents pays tribute to all of America's chiefs of state. George Washington, honored with the greatest number of portraits, has a separate gallery devoted to him to display the multitude of interpretations: the first President is youthful and majestic, mature and bewigged, crowned by angels, set in marble and draped in a Roman toga and, of course, painted by Gilbert Stuart.

Statesmen and admirals, Revolutionary heroes, patriots and generals have their fair share of space on these hallowed halls. But Americans have distinguished themselves in many fields: sports and music, education and industry, medicine and philosophy. Here also are the men and women who have flown heroically into uncharted skies, written books that have spurred social reform, built inventions that have irrevocably changed our lives. Here are entertainers who have sung and danced for us, actors who have helped us laugh and weep. Here too are the charismatic leaders, the inspiring poets, the thinkers and the artists.

Yet these halls are not entirely filled with heroes. Surprisingly, but fitting the Gallery's mandate to portray people 'significant' to the history of the United States, a place is made for a number of scoundrels and villains. Jay Gould can be found, the railroad speculator who manipulated the gold market in 1869, causing the Black Friday panic. Benedict Arnold, Revolutionary soldier-turned-traitor, is remembered as well. In an ironic turn, John Wilkes Booth and Lee Harvey Oswald share space in this museum with the presidents they assassinated.

Naturalized citizens are as welcome in this place as native sons and daughters, and expatriates return home once again. Albert Einstein and George Gershwin, Babe Ruth and T S Eliot, Golda Meir and Amelia Earhart are but a few of the diverse men and women who have left their mark on America and the world. These are the men and women who have shaped history.

Right This photograph was made on April 10, 1865, in the studio of Washington photographer Alexander Gardner, four days before Abraham Lincoln was assassinated, and is the last known picture of the Great Emancipator (photograph albumen silver-print, NPG.81.M1)

Osceola, 1838
George Catlin
Oil on canvas, 30¾ × 25¾ inches
(78 × 65.4 cm)
On loan from National Museum of
American Art (L/NPG.7.70)

George Catlin travelled through the
American wilderness during the 1830s
to paint the 'vanishing races of native
man in America.' He painted scenes of
buffalo hunts, religious ceremonies,
and daily life among the Indians. He
also made many portraits of Native
Americans, some – like Chief
Osceola, shown here – well-known
and others known only because Catlin
painted them. When Catlin tried to
sell his collection to Congress to pre-

serve it for the American people,
many felt that not one penny of public
funds should be spent on paintings of
mere savages. After Catlin's death,
Congress did authorize funds to purchase his collection, much of which is
now in the National Gallery and the
National Portrait Gallery.

This painting shows Osceola, a
leader among the Seminole Indians of
Florida, who led a revolt to protest his
people's forced relocation. In 1837
Osceola, carrying a white flag of
truce, entered Fort Augustine to
negotiate peace. He was at once captured and imprisoned in Fort Moul-
trie, South Carolina. Osceola died in
captivity the next year shortly after
Catlin painted this portrait.

Thomas Alva Edison, c.1889
Abraham Archibald Anderson
Oil on canvas, 44¾ × 54½ inches
(113.5 × 138.5 cm)
Transfer from the NMAA; Gift of Dr
Eleanor Campbell to the Smithsonian
Institution (NPG.65.23)

This oil portrait shows the American
inventor Thomas Edison (1847-1931)
at the Paris University Exposition of
1889, listening to the famous 'first
perfected phonograph' which he had
patented in 1878. Few Americans
changed the way their fellow citizens
lived to the extent that Edison did.
Born in Ohio in 1847, Edison had

only three months of formal schooling
before his mother pulled him out of
school at age seven after a teacher criti-
cized the lad's constant classroom
questions. The teacher mistook young
Thomas's questions as a sign of incom-
prehension whereas, of course, the
questions were a sign of Edison's lively
and curious mind. Self-taught, Edison
went on to turn night into day with the
incandescent electric light bulb, and
more than 1300 other patented inventions. Known for his inventive genius
as 'The Wizard', Edison's legacy includes the dictaphone, paraffin paper,
the automatic telegraph system and a
motion picture camera.

Tallulah B Bankhead, 1930
Augustus John
Oil on canvas, 48 × 24½ inches
(122.9 × 62.7 cm)
Gift of the Hon. and Mrs John Hay
Whitney (NPG.69.46)

There was a day when this lady
needed no introduction. Indeed, she is
one of those special historical charac-
ters who are known only by their first
name; there was, and probably always
will be, only one Tallulah. The
daughter of a prominent Alabama
politician – he was a member of the
US House of Representatives from
1917-1940, its Speaker from 1936-40 –
she made her debut on Broadway
when only 16 and within a few years
was as much a presence on the
London stage and scene as on Broadway and in New York. By 1931 she
was also making movies. Not until
her 1939 appearance in Lillian Hell-
man's *The Little Foxes,* though, did
she begin to gain true critical respect.
Thereafter she played a number of
notable parts on stage and in films,
eventually also appearing on television. But perhaps her greatest role
was as herself: her striking looks, her
deep voice, her brassy manner, her
blunt talk, her free-spirited life, all
made her the media's favorite 'Dah-
'ling,' as she was fond of calling
everyone. No single portrait could
hope to capture all of Tallulah, but
this portrait by the great English
painter Augustus John comes close.

Amelia Earhart, early 1930s
Edith A Scott
Oil on canvas,
(NPG.75.82)

The adventurous aviatrix Amelia Earhart (1898-1937) was a modest
heroine. Edith Scott's portrait of the
heroic Earhart emphasized the unas-
suming bravery of the subject, who
posed wearing her dashing leather
flight jacket. Earhart was first lauded
for her courage in 1928 when she became the first woman to fly – but only
as a passenger – across the Atlantic.
Earhart downplayed her role, com-
menting wryly: 'The bravest thing I
did was try to drop a bag of oranges
and a note on the head of an ocean
liner's captain – and I missed the
whole ship.' But four years later Earhart crossed the Atlantic in a dange-
rous 15-hour solo flight, an important
first for a woman. Not stopping to
bask in her new glory, she followed
this achievement by becoming the
first woman to fly non-stop across
America. When not flying, Earhart
worked as student adviser for women
at Purdue University and wrote
several books, including *The Fun of It*
about her aviation adventures. Earhart's last flight ended in disaster:
while attempting to circumnavigate
the globe in 1937, she and her navigator disappeared over the Pacific.

Left above
Self-Portrait, 1934
George Gershwin
Oil on canvas board, 15¾ × 11¾ inches
(39.9 × 29.8 cm)
Gift of Ira Gershwin (NPG.66.48)

One of America's greatest compos-
ers, George Gershwin was born in
Brooklyn in 1898. His one-of-a-kind
style blended folk music with traditional forms, creating wonderful, sur-
prising shifts in harmony and
rhythm. At the age of 25, Gershwin
wrote the renowned symphonic jazz
composition, *Rhapsody in Blue*. Following a string of Broadway successes, in 1931 he won a Pulitzer Prize
for his score of the comedy *Of Thee I
Sing*. His final work, written shortly
before he died of a brain tumor at age
38, was *Porgy and Bess*, a folk opera of
black America. Gershwin relaxed
while writing the score for *Porgy and
Bess* by painting this self-portrait in
1934. He chose to show himself as
composer and pianist, his hand rest-
ong on the piano keys, his profile in
front of a fresh musical score.

Left below
Paul Bustill Robeson, 1924
Winold Reiss
Pastel on artboard, 30¹/₁₆ × 21⁹/₁₆ inches
(76.3 × 54.8 cm)
Gift of Lawrence A Fleischman and
Howard Garfinkle with a matching
grant from NEA (NPG.72.80)

The brilliant – he was a lawyer before
he went on the stage – black actor and
concert singer Paul Robeson had a
controversial career. After appearing
in 1924 in Eugene O'Neill's *Emperor
Jones*, and in Jerome Kern's *Show Boat*
in 1928, Robeson became an international star when he appeared as *Oth-
ello* both in the United States and
abroad. Yet, just as his career seemed
assured, Robeson became increas-
ingly concerned with social injustice.
Because of his activities, Robeson was
hounded by the US government and
he moved to the USSR in 1950, where
he was awarded the Stalin Peace prize.
He was permitted to return to the
United States in the 1960s, and saw
some of the changes for which he had
fought taking place in society. This
portrait by Winold Reiss clearly
shows Robeson's forceful person-
ality.

Golda Meir, 1975
Raphael Soyer
Oil on canvas, 32 × 26 inches
(81.5 × 66 cm)
Gift of Mr and Mrs Nathan Cummings,
Mr and Mrs Myer P Potamkins and the
Charles E Smith Family Foundation
(NPG.75.81)

Both the painter and the subject of this painting were born in Russia and emigrated to the United States. In 1921 Golda Meir moved once again, this time to Palestine, with her husband Morris Meyerson (later Hebraicized to 'Meir'). At the height of a success-ful political career Golda, as everyone called her, became Israel's first (and thus far only) woman Prime Minister in 1969. Her no-nonsense attitude in negotiations, political savvy, and warmth made Golda an enormously popular figure in Israel.

CHAPTER NINE

Arthur M Sackler Gallery

Not only is Asian art exceptional for its beauty, diversity and technical skill, it is also remarkable for its great antiquity. For the past 5000 years, jade has inspired artists in China. An extremely difficult mineral to work, jade is sliced with abrasives and sculpted, decorated and polished using simple grinding tools. Since ancient times, the techniques used to produce intricate objects have remained largely unchanged.

Chinese bronzes reached an unparalleled technical perfection during the Bronze Age which began in the Shang dynasty (c. 1700 BC–c. 1050 BC). Ritual wine and water containers and cooking vessels were cast in many shapes, with decorative motifs including dragons, birds and other animals. Often buried with the dead, they were probably meant as offerings to spirits of nature, such as mountains and rivers, as well as to deceased ancestors.

The art of the Ancient Near East also dates to remote antiquity, with fine metalwork produced as early as the third millennium BC. In Iran, artists created powerful aesthetic works over a timespan of thousands of years, depicting traditional subjects such as mythological beasts, horses, cattle and dancing women. The pieces were created by sophisticated methods such as casting, hammering, gilding and repoussé; royal objects were made from gold and silver, while common utilitarian wares were usually modeled in clay or cast in bronze.

Examples of these fine arts of antiquity from the Near East, China, India and South-east Asia form the heart of the Arthur M Sackler Gallery. The foundation of the museum's collection was a gift of 1000 prized works donated in 1982 by the late Dr Arthur M Sackler, a medical researcher and art connoisseur. In offering the gift, Dr Sackler set terms that were generous almost beyond imagination: a representative of the Smithsonian would be permitted to choose fifty million dollars' worth of objects from his extensive collection. Ultimately, when the value was tallied, the philanthropist set no limits.

Although he had been collecting Impressionist paintings and pre-Columbian ceramics for nearly a decade, Dr Sackler's interests turned in 1950 toward the Asian works that now fill the gallery bearing his name. 'I collect as a biologist,' he said. 'To really understand a civilization or society, you must have a large enough corpus data.' This idea is reflected in his gift to the Smithsonian, which includes objects crafted and painted from antiquity to contemporary times.

The Arthur M Sackler Gallery opened in 1987 as part of the new underground Quadrangle complex. With its pyramidal copper-clad roofs and diamond-shaped windows and designs, the entrance pavilion suggests the perfect symmetry that is found in many Asian art objects. Inside the museum, the works are displayed in galleries that use traditional Oriental architectural motifs and cabinetry.

Chinese art, created in several media, predominates here. The large jade collection spans the vast period from c. 3000 BC to 1700 AD and includes early utilitarian jade axes and blades as well as many delicate, whimsical pieces in the form of birds, dragons and fantastic animals. Chinese paintings are represented through wall paintings on stucco produced as early as the seventh century AD, traditional landscapes dating from the fourteenth to eighteenth centuries, and recent scrolls by twentieth-century artists. A magnificent group of lacquerware boxes and dishes comes from China as well.

The arts of Indian and South-east Asia – often inseparable from spiritual devotion – are represented through religious sculptures of the tenth to fourteenth centuries AD. In those regions, stone figures of Hindu gods and goddesses covered the outsides of temples, sometimes by the thousand, symbolizing the infinite aspects of divinity and life. The collection includes examples of granite and sandstone images, as well as bronze figures that were kept on temple altars or in household shrines.

The Sackler Gallery's Henri Vever Collection is a vibrant group of 500 Persian, Indian and Turkish works that include paintings, manuscripts, illuminations and bookbindings. In opulent colors, they illustrate tales of royal princes and princesses, marriages, battles, demons, and adventures from classical Persian texts and Arabian works.

The Sackler complements the Smithsonian's Freer Gallery and shares staff and research facilities with it. Together, the two museums bring the rich artistic and cultural traditions of Asia to the American public.

Right The entrance pavilion to the Arthur M Sackler Gallery prepares visitors for the Asian art they are about to view.

Left
Bronze Bell, 1200–1100 BC
Shang Period
Chinese metalwork, 12¹³⁄₁₆ × 9¾ ×
6 inches (32.6 × 24.9 × 15.4 cm)
(S.1987.10)

This *zhong*, or ritual bell, exhibits the technical perfection characteristic of so many of the large variety of bronze ritual objects from the Bronze Age in China, particularly of the Shang dynasty, (c. 1766–1050 BC) when this was made. In addition to the crested birds atop the bell and the large hooked flanges along the sides, what immediately engages the viewer is the decorative element in the center, a *taotie* mask. This motif, so popular in the Shang dynasty, is a stylized face with shapes suggesting large eyes and ears and often fangs and horns. Eactly what this motif meant to Chinese of the period is not known. A bronze bell such as this was probably not meant for practical use; more likely it was used as an offering to spirits of nature or was a symbol of authority. Such bells were then buried in the tombs of royalty and the aristocracy, and are believed to have been used in rituals connected with the spirits of the dead.

Above
Ding (ritual cooking vessel),
700–600 BC
Eastern Zhou dynasty, Spring
and Autumn period
Chinese metalwork, 13⁹⁄₁₆ × 14⁹⁄₁₆ ×
12⅛ inches (34.5 × 37.1 × 31.1 cm)
(S1987.326)

Many of the variety of shapes displayed by ancient Chinese bronze ritual vessels were based on traditional pottery forms originating in the late Neolithic era (c. 5000–c.1700 BC). Such vessels included wine containers and warmers, water basins, food containers and food cookers. An example of the last named is this three-legged, shallow-bowled *ding* from the Eastern Zhou dynasty, seventh century BC. The Zhou dynasty, traditionally known in the West as the Chou Dynasty, was China's second dynasty, which overthrew the first, the Shang, and ruled from 1122–221 BC. The Zhou dynasty never really gained much control over its eastern territories. The decoration of such bronze vessels evolved from narrow geometric bands to the type seen here: ornate patterns using motifs such as interlocking dragons and birds and, on the lower band, *taotie* mask designs. Such fine bronze vessels were almost certainly designed for rituals, not for ordinary cooking.

Right above
Chinese bottle/water dropper,
c.200–400 AD
Six Dynasties
Jade, 2⅛ × 6⅜ × 3 inches
(5.4 × 16.4 × 7.7 cm)
(S.1987.796)

Despite its fantastic appearance, this jade creature, which belonged to a Chinese scholar in the Six Dynasties period, (third to fourth centuries AD), served a useful purpose. When water was poured into the opening on the animal's neck, an internal reservoir filled and drops of water flowed into the tiny bowl held in the mouth. There it would mix with the ground ink pigment used for calligraphy, the fine handwriting that has always been highly honored in China. Jade artists in China have been practicing their craft for 5000 years. The mineral stone known as jade (although modern mineralogists regard only jadeite and nephrite as true jade, the Chinese also consider a number of other minerals as jade) is usually a very hard material; and to shape it with such artistry requires great skill.

Right below
Horn Rhyton, c.300–400 AD
Sassanian
Metalwork, silver and gilt,
6⅛ × 10 × 5⁹⁄₁₆ × 5½ inches
(15.7 × 25.6 × 14.1 × 14 cm)
(S.1987.33)

This silver and gold drinking vessel is a superb example of a rhyton, the Greek term for all such vessels in the general shape of a horn and with the tip or end having the features of an animal, human or mythological creature. The originals were decorated animal horns; then came ceramic versions, with ends formed to represent animals or other beings; finally came the more elaborate metal rhytons such as this. All reflected the same idea of drinking liquids as they issued from the mouth of another being. This particular rhyton is believed to come from Iran and to date from about the fourth century AD. The head, both sensitive and powerful, is that of a goat. In the center of the flaring base (not visible here) is a three-branched tree; flanking it are two antelopes, and beside them are a lion (seen here) and a bull.

Above
Stag 1–1000 AD, Turkestan
Copper alloy, 22 × 18¼ × 12¾ inches
(56.3 × 46.7 × 32.6 cm)
(S.1987.119)

Among the more imposing of the many fine pieces from the ancient Near East in the Sackler Gallery is this fabulous stag made of copper alloy. Although standing only 22 inches high, it makes an almost monumental impact because of the sheer virtuosity of the antlers, themselves some 18 inches wide. Although the stag's body is not precisely realistic, it is clearly the work of someone who has observed this animal; with the head, though, the maker seems to abandon any attempt at realism, and the protruding tongue and earring complete the fanciful aspect. The antlers are so vigorous and expressive that they might almost be viewed as a separate work, and indeed are affixed to the head by a skull cap that is attached by an L-shaped piece of metal.

Unfortunately, little is known of this piece's exact provenance, but it is reliably assumed to have been made in Central Asia sometime within the first thousand years of the modern era. The tradition in that part of the world of making such metal animals, particularly stags with exaggerated antlers, goes back to at least 2500 BC. Just what purpose such figures served is not known for sure, but the assumption is that they played some role in the religious life of their creators. But was the figure itself used in some ritual? Was the stag itself revered? No one knows for sure. What even the casual visitor to a museum can appreciate, however, is the sense of power and wonder communicated by these prominent, even threatening, antlers.

Left
Bodhisattva and Dark-Skinned Figure,
Chinese Chin-Song period,
975-1025 AD
Pigment on stucco, 69⅛ × 33⅝ inches
(176.9 × 86 cm)
(S.1987.224)

Originally part of a larger work, this painting on stucco probably came from the interior of a Buddhist temple in China. In this fragment we see a *bodhisattva* – a being on the path to enlightenment who forsakes Nirvana so that he may save others by leading them on the spiritual way of Buddha – blessing a dark-skinned figure. The halos around the heads of both suggest that they are equally spiritual beings.

Above
Octagonal Box with Qiangjin Decoration, 1279-1368 AD
Chinese, Yuan dynasty
Lacquer and gold on wood, 6⅞ × 7 × 7¹⁄₁₆ inches (17.5 × 17.9 × 18.1 cm)
(S.1987.224)

This delicate little octagonal box is from China and is dated to the Yuan dynasty, the period when China fell under the harsh rule of the Mongols from the north, led by Kublai Khan. (It was during this time, 1275-1292, that Marco Polo visited China.) The box is wood and is made in three separate parts: the base, the central section, and the lid. It was probably made in the fourteenth century and, since it required considerable care and expense to make, most likely

belonged to a member of the aristocracy, possibly a Mongol overlord. The workmanship, however, is distinctly Chinese and employs a technique known as *qiangjin*. A red-pigmented lacquer is first applied to the exterior of the box (the interior has a plain black lacquer); then lines and designs, here derived from peonies, are engraved into the lacquer and filled with gold leaf. Lacquer is made from the sap of a tree, usually the *Rhus verniciflus*; applied in thin layers, it builds up to a glossy varnish-like surface that is highly resistant to both moisture and air. Lacquer has been used in China since about 3500 BC and by the time of the Song dynasty (906-1279 AD) more elaborate techniques such as *qiangjin* were being applied to lacquered surfaces.

Left
Siva Sukhasanamurti,
1100–1300 AD
South India
Cast bronze, 27 × 15½ × 13⅞ inches
(69.1 × 39.7 × 35.5 cm)
(S.1987.911)

In India, bronze images of Hindu gods and goddesses have traditionally been placed on temple altars or in household shrines. This thirteenth/ fourteenth century figure of Shiva, the god of destruction, was part of a *Somaskandha* group which also contained Shiva's consort, Uma, and their son Skandha, the god of war. (The term *somaskandha* is formed from combining parts of these three deities' names *sa + uma = soma + skandha*.) Shiva's lower hand forms the peace sign and his upper hand originally held a small deer. Shiva (or Siva) is one of the two chief deities of the Hindu religion, the other being Vishnu. Although he can be terrifying and is known as 'The Destroyer,' that is because he periodically destroys the world in order to re-create it; he is also regarded as being merciful, and this particular image seems to embody that more benign aspect.

Above
The Court of Gayumarth,
1518 AD
Folio 212, *Shahnama* of Abu'l-Qasim Firdawsi, Iran, Shiraz
Opaque watercolor, ink and gold on paper, 6⅞ × 3½ inches (17.5 × 8.9 cm)
(S.1986.58)

This delicate illustration adorns a page from a copy (dated to 1518) of the *Shahnama* (Book of Kings), the Iranian epic poem by Abu'l-Qasim Firdawsi. It shows the mythological progenitor of humankind and the first king of Persia (Iran), Gayumarth, seated on an animal skin and surrounded by his court, many of whom wear leopardskin clothes. Firdawsi (932–1026 AD) is still regarded as one of the greatest of Iranian poets and his *Shahnama* as one of the greatest Persian epics; over the centuries it was handcopied and illustrated in many similarly fine volumes. This page was acquired in the early part of the twentieth century by the Parisian jeweler, art collector and painter, Henri Vever; when he died in 1942 his fabulous collection of Islamic art from the Middle East and Asia vanished for many years but was eventually acquired by the Smithsonian with help from Dr Arthur M Sackler.

Index

Acknowledgments

The publisher would like to thank
David Eldred, who designed this
book; Rita Longabucco for picture
research; Helen Jarvis for the index;
and Sherry Marker for assistance
with captions. We would also like to
thank the following individuals,
agencies and institutions for
supplying illustrations.
Arthur M Sackler Gallery: pages
150, 151, 152, 153 (both), 154, 155,
156, 157
The Bettmann Archive: pages 6,
11 (bottom), 12 (both), 13 (bottom),
15 (bottom), 24-25, 76, 77, 128
FPG International: pages 90
(photo M Kaufman), 127 (P Beney),
130 (F Dole)
Freer Gallery of Art: pages 4, 11

(top), 95 (both), 96, 97, 98, 99, 100,
101, 102, 103, 104, 105 (both)
**Hirshhorn Museum and
Sculpture Garden** (photo New
England Stock, Barbara Moore):
page 108; (photo Lee Stalsworth):
pages 2, 109, 110, 111, 112, 113, 114,
115, 116, 117, 118, 119, 120, 121,
122-23, 124, 125
National Museum of African Art,
Eliot Eliofson Archives: pages 16,
17, 18, 19 (both), 20 (all photos
Jeffrey Ploskonka), 21 (photo Bruce
Fleischer)
**National Museum of American
Art:** 1, 46, 46-47, 48, 49, 50-51,
52-53, 54, 55, 56, 57, 58, 59, 60, 61,
62, 63, 64-65, 66-67, 70, 71, 72, 73
(both)

National Portrait Gallery: pages
141, 142, 143, 144 (photo Eugene L
Mantie), 145, 146 (both), 147
New England Stock (photo 32, 33,
34, 36, 37, 38, 39, 40, 41, 42, 43, 45,
78, 79, 80, 81, 82, 83, 84, 85 (both),
86 (bottom), 87, 91, 92, 93 (both),
107, 108, 131, 132, 133 (both), 134,
136-37, 139 (right); (photo Jim
Schwabel): pages 9, 15 (top), 23, 68,
74, 86 (top), 88; (photo Jackie
Linder): pages 10, 149
Ron Schramm: page 7
**Smithsonian Institution,
Photographic Services:** pages 13
(top), 28, 29 (top), 30, 35, 135, 138
(both), 139 (left)